BIG ENGLISH ③

T0345775

Contents

unit 1 Wake Up!

1 **What's missing in the pictures? Match and write.**

do   eat   play

1

a  She _____ in the morning.

2

b  She _____ in the afternoon.

3

c  She _____ after school.

2 **Read and circle.**

1 wake **up** / **off**

2 go **home** / **to home**

3 go to **park** / **the park**

4 go **school** / **to school**

5 **get** / **go** dressed

6 **watch** / **see** TV

3 Listen and write. Then match.

Hurry, Kate!

a

It's Monday, ¹____.
Kate has to wake up.
Her mom sees the clock and says
Wake up, sleepy head.

Go, go, go! Hurry, Kate!
Hurry, Kate! You can't be late!

Kate eats breakfast, she gets dressed.
It's ²____.
It's time to go to school.
And she can't be late!

Chorus

Kate has her backpack
And she has her lunch.
What time is it now?
Oh, no, it's time to go!

Chorus

b

---

4 Find out. Answer and draw. When does your friend wake up?

_____

_____

---

5 Read and circle.

1 seven o'clock   **a** 7:00   **b** 6:00

2 five twenty-five   **a** 2:25   **b** 5:25

3 four forty-five   **a** 4:05   **b** 4:45

4 two thirty   **a** 2:30   **b** 2:13

6 **Read. Write T for true and F for false.**

I Love Mondays!

It's Monday and Luke wakes up. He says, "Hooray! I love Mondays!" On Mondays, he has art at 11:10 before lunch. After lunch, at 2:15, he has English. After school, he plays soccer or basketball. Luke eats breakfast and gets dressed. He puts on his shoes. He's ready for school, but today there's no school. It's a holiday!

1 Today is Monday.   _____   **2** Luke has art after school.   _____

3 He has English before lunch.   _____   **4** He's ready for school.   _____

5 He plays soccer after school.   _____   **6** He goes to school today.   _____

7 **Write about you. What do you do before school and after school?**

1 Before school, _____.

2 After school, _____.

THINK BIG

What does Luke do next? Draw and write.

Luke _____

_____

_____.

10

8 **Listen and stick. Number the pictures and answer.**

a

When does she go to bed?

_____

b

When does she go to school?

_____

c

When does she eat breakfast?

_____

d

When does she wake up?

_____

9 **Correct the sentences for you.**

1 I do my homework in the morning.

_____

2 I eat breakfast at 9:30.

_____

3 I go home at 4:45.

_____

4 I play basketball after school.

_____

5 I watch TV in the morning, afternoon, and evening.

_____

10 **Read. Then write before or after.**

wakes up

eats breakfast

gets dressed

goes to school

does homework

watches TV

goes to bed

1 Susan eats breakfast _____ she wakes up.

2 She wakes up _____ she gets dressed.

3 She gets dressed _____ she goes to school.

4 She does her homework _____ she goes to school.

5 She does her homework _____ she watches TV.

6 She goes to bed _____ she does her homework.

11 **Write the answers.**

1 What does your brother or sister do before school?

_____

2 What does your brother or sister do after school?

_____

3 What does your mom or dad do before school?

_____

4 What does your mom or dad do after school?

_____

12 **Look and complete the chart.**

> bath   face   hair   hands   shower   teeth

have/take a	wash your	brush your	brush/comb your

12

13 **Listen and write. Then match the pictures a–c to paragraphs 1–3.**

> Bacteria   decay   Dirty   shower   sneeze   wash

1   It's important that we are clean every day. We can take a bath or a ¹ _____. We always have to use warm water to ² _____ away dirt, sweat, dead skin, and bacteria. Bacteria are very, very small and live on our skin. We can't see them, but they can make us sick.

a

2   We have to brush our teeth every day for about two minutes. Brush them in the morning and before you go to bed. ³ _____ can cause tooth ⁴ _____ and gum disease, so brushing our teeth keeps them strong and healthy.

b

3   We have to keep our hands clean, too. ⁵ _____ hands have germs that make us sick. We need to wash our hands with soap before we eat, after we go to the bathroom, or when we cough or ⁶ _____.

c

14 **Find and write the words.**

ieraacbt

iseedas

trydi

1 _____

2 _____

3 _____

swtea

sgrem

4 _____

5 _____

15 **Read and match.**

1 We brush our	water and soap	to wash away bacteria.
2 We use	hands	after we cough or sneeze.
3 We wash our	teeth	to stop gum disease.

16 **Put the words in order.**

1 | germs | leaves | Coughing | on our hands. |

_____

2 | full | germs. | Sneezes | of | are |

_____

3 | hands. | clean | our | soap | water | Warm | and |

_____

4 | teeth | your | decay. | Brushing | tooth | stops |

_____

THINK BIG **Where can you find germs? Put a ✓ or a ✗.**

☐ In the bathroom ☐ In the yard ☐ In the park

17 **Look at the chart. Circle T for true and F for false.**

	Linda	Jose	Melissa
Play basketball	5	3	5
Take a shower	3	1	4
Eat healthy food	4	2	2
Take the bus to school	1	5	3
Go to bed before 10 p.m.	2	4	5

1 Always   2 Usually   3 Often   4 Sometimes   5 Never

1   Linda usually goes to bed before 10 p.m.   **T**   **F**

2   Melissa often takes the bus to school.   **T**   **F**

3   Melissa always takes a shower.   **T**   **F**

4   Linda never eats healthy food.   **T**   **F**

5   Jose often plays basketball.   **T**   **F**

6   Jose and Melissa usually eat healthy food.   **T**   **F**

18 **Look at 17. Make sentences with always, usually, often, sometimes, or never.**

1   Linda and Melissa/play basketball

_____

2   Jose/take a shower

_____

3   Melissa/eat healthy food

_____

4   Jose and Melissa/eat healthy food

_____

5   Linda/take the bus to school

_____

6   Jose/go to bed before 10 p.m.

_____

Grammar

19 **Make questions.**

1 you/sometimes/walk to school

_____? Yes, I do.

2 she/always/brush her teeth

_____? No, she doesn't.

3 they/usually/play in the park

_____? Yes, they do.

4 your dad/often/eat cereal for breakfast

_____? Yes, he does.

20 **Make negative sentences.**

1 I always play computer games.

_____

2 We often eat pasta for lunch.

_____

3 Sometimes I walk the dog.

_____

4 She often cleans her room.

_____

5 He usually goes to bed early.

_____

21 **Read and complete.**

away   of   on   to   with

1 We have to get rid _____ germs.

2 Bacteria live _____ our skin and in our mouth.

3 You have to wash _____ soap and water.

4 We need _____ stay clean and healthy.

5 We can wash the dirt _____ in the shower.

22 **Look at the times. Complete.**

New York
Manuel

Texas
Maria

Montana
John

California
Kara

1 It's one fifteen in New York. What time is it in Texas? _____

2 It's eleven fifteen in Montana. What time is it in California? _____

3 It's ten fifteen. Where am I? _____

4 It's twelve fifteen. Where am I? _____

23 **Listen and circle.**

1 Time isn't the same around the world. We live on a **¹ globe / circle** with different time **² days / zones**. For example, when it's day in Hong Kong, it's night in New York. When there's sun in New Zealand, it's dark in the U.K. Often these places are in a different **³ day / week**, too.

2 This is because the **⁴ Earth / Moon** makes half a full turn every 12 hours. This means New York sees its new day 12 hours after Hong Kong. There are often different **⁵ time / night** zones in the same country, too, such as in Russia or in the U.S.A. The U.S.A. has four **⁶ different / big** time zones.

3 For example, when it's 10:30 a.m. for Kara in California, she's in class. She's had breakfast, so she isn't hungry yet. But John in Montana is getting hungry because it's 11:30 a.m. He wants his **⁷ breakfast / lunch** soon! It's already lunch time for Maria in Texas, where it's 12:30 p.m. And lunch is finished for Manuel, because the time in New York is 1:30 p.m.

24 **Look at 23. Circle T for true and F for false.**

1 We have night and day because the Earth turns.   T   F

2 All countries have the same time zones.   T   F

3 The U.S.A. is in the same time zone as Hong Kong.   T   F

4 Countries can be in different days because of time zones.   T   F

5 When it's 10:30 in California, it's 12:30 in New York.   T   F

6 When Manuel has finished lunch, John is getting hungry.   T   F

25 **Write the times using words.**

1 (10:10/London) _____.

2 (12:30/Paris) _____.

3 (18:00/Cairo) _____.

4 (17:25/Beijing) _____.

5 (21:45/Tokyo) _____.

26 **Read and answer.**

It's 1:00 a.m. in London. What time is it in...

1 Los Angeles (-8 hours) _____   5 Moscow (+3 hours) _____

2 Mexico City (-6 hours) _____   6 Singapore (+7 hours) _____

3 Boston (-5 hours) _____   7 Sydney (+11 hours) _____

4 Istanbul (+2 hours) _____   8 Buenos Aires (-4 hours) _____

THINK BIG **Do you know anyone who lives in another time zone? Where are they? What's the time difference?**

Name: _____   Lives: _____

Time difference: + / - _____ hours

27 **How many subjects and how many verbs can you find?**

Julie wakes up at 6:45. Then she eats breakfast. She washes her face. She brushes her teeth. She gets dressed. She goes to school at 8:30.

28 **Underline the subject.**

1 Jeff wakes up at 6:45 in the morning.

2 We go to school at 7:30 in the morning.

3 I feed my cat before school.

4 Carol does the dishes in the evening.

5 He plays basketball in the afternoon.

29 **Underline the verb.**

1 I make my bed before school.

2 He rides his bike to school.

3 They play video games after school.

4 My sister reads books every day.

5 My sister comes home at 3:45.

30 **Write about three family members. What do they do?**

Family Members			
My aunt	My brother	My cousin	My father
My mother	My sister	My uncle	

1 _____ in the morning.

2 _____ in the afternoon.

3 _____ in the evening.

31 **Read and circle a_e, i_e, and o_e.**

face

bone

sheep

time

bike

soup

cake

note

32 **Underline the words with a_e, i_e, and o_e. Then read aloud.**

1 The girl is eating a cake and the dog is eating a bone.

2 I love my bike and my board game.

33 **Connect the letters. Then write.**

1 f   one   **a** _ _ _ _

2 l   ace   **b** _ _ _ _

3 b   ike   **c** _ _ _ _

20

34 **Listen and write.**

What time is it?

It's time to play a ¹_____.

What time is it?

It's time to eat ²_____.

What time is it?

It's time to ride a ³_____.

What time is it?

It's time to go ⁴_____.

35 **Match and write sentences for you. Use before or after.**

1 wash my   **a** a shower   _____

2 wash   **b** my teeth   _____

3 take   **c** face   _____

4 brush   **d** hair   _____

5 comb my   **e** my hands   _____

36 **Put the words in order. Find out and then answer.**

1 does | When | wake | your dad | up? | usually

_____

_____

2 When | her hands? | does | wash | your mom

_____

_____

3 bed | your parents | Do | go to | always | at 9 p.m.?

_____

_____

4 it | What | is | time | now?

_____

_____

5 you | watch TV | sometimes | Do | on Saturday?

_____

_____

A Lot of Jobs!

1 Follow the paths and write the jobs.

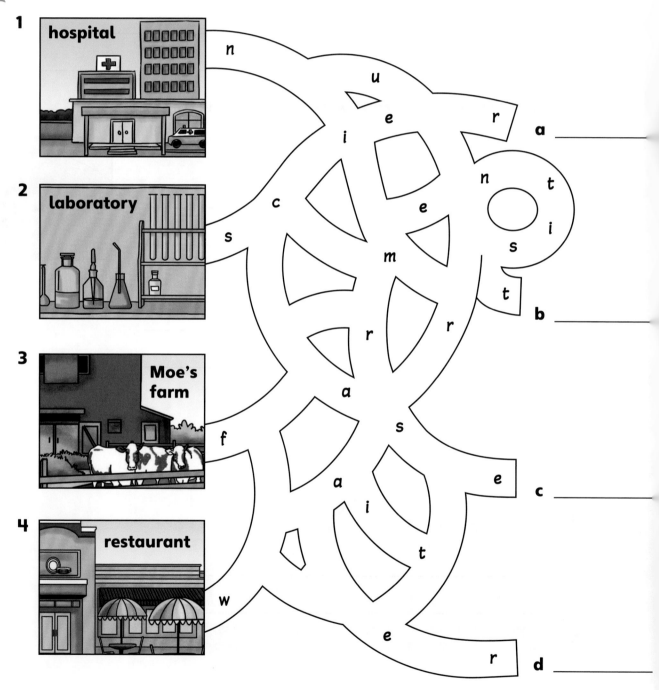

1 hospital

2 laboratory

3 Moe's farm

4 restaurant

a _____

b _____

c _____

d _____

2 Listen and number in order from 1–5. Then circle all the jobs.

Working Together

Working together, working hard.
Nurse, farmer, teacher, and chef.

Where does he work?
What does he do?
He's a firefighter,
And he's very brave, too.

There are many people
In our community.
So many jobs to do,
So many places to be.

Where does she work?
What does she do?
She's a nurse,
And she always helps you.

Working together, working hard.
Nurse, farmer, teacher, and chef.

3 Read and circle **T** for true and **F** for false.

1	A firefighter works on a farm.	T	F
2	A waiter works at a restaurant.	T	F
3	A police officer works at a store.	T	F
4	A student studies at a college.	T	F
5	A cashier works at a laboratory.	T	F

4 Choose a job and draw. Then answer.

What does he/she do?

_____

_____

Where does he/she work?

_____

_____

5 **Read. Then circle.**

Is She a Doctor?

Luke and his dad are at the hospital. They are looking for Luke's mom. Luke's mom works at the hospital. But she isn't a doctor. She's a cashier. She works in the hospital gift shop. Today's her birthday!

1 Luke is looking for **a nurse** / **his mom**.

2 Luke's mom works at the **post office** / **hospital**.

3 Luke's mom is a **doctor** / **cashier**.

4 She works in the **gift shop** / **supermarket**.

6 **Answer the questions about a family member.**

  1 What does he or she do? _____

  2 Where does he or she work? _____

THINK BIG

How does Luke's mom celebrate her birthday? What does she do? Draw and write.

_____

_____

_____

29

7 Listen and stick. Then number.

a

□

b

□

c

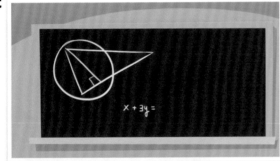

□

8 Look and complete.

1 A: What ¹_____ your brothers ²_____?

B: They ³_____ firefighters.

A: Where ⁴_____ they work?

B: They ⁵_____ at the ⁶_____.

2 A: What ¹_____ your dad ²_____?

B: He ³_____ a waiter.

A: Where ⁴_____ he ⁵_____?

B: He ⁶_____ at a Spanish ⁷_____.

Language in Action

9 **Listen and ✓.**

1 What does Peggy's dad do?

He's ☐ a cashier. ☐ a teacher. ☐ a farmer.

2 Where does Peggy's mom work?

She works ☐ at a restaurant. ☐ at a police station. ☐ at a fire station.

3 Where does Peggy's brother work?

He works ☐ at a laboratory. ☐ at a college. ☐ at a school.

4 What does her sister do?

She's ☐ a chef. ☐ a student. ☐ a police officer.

10 **Read and write Where or What.**

1 **A:** _____ does your brother work?
B: He works at a post office.

2 **A:** _____ does your sister do?
B: She's a nurse.

3 **A:** _____ do you do?
B: I'm a scientist.

4 **A:** _____ do your parents work?
B: They work on a farm.

11 **Put the words in order.**

1 does | uncle | What | do? | your

_____

2 waiter. | He's | a

_____

3 at | He | a | works | restaurant.

_____

12 **Read and match.**

 a    b    c

1 Susie is a fashion designer.

2 Jake is an artist.

3 Mark is a photographer.

33

13 **Listen, read, and complete.**

> camera   creative   fashion   galleries   job   sketches   work

1   We spend a lot of time at ¹ _____, so it's important to choose a ² _____ we enjoy. Here are some creative jobs.

2   Professional artists study first at art school. They learn to be ³ _____ with different materials. Artists draw with pencils, or paint with oil paints, acrylics, or watercolors. They sometimes use metal or wood to make other works of art. Some artists use unusual materials like chewing gum, buttons, or even plastic supermarket bags! Artists show their work in ⁴ _____.

3   Photographers take pictures of people, places, and things all over the world. Good photographers always have a ⁵ _____ with them. They sell their pictures to websites, newspapers, magazines, and television news shows. Their pictures are also used in books.

4   Fashion designers design the clothes we wear. They have good ideas and draw ⁶ _____ of them. Then they cut patterns to make clothes, such as dresses, pants, or coats. We see their work in ⁷ _____ shows or at photo shoots for magazines. We can buy their clothes in shops or online.

14 **Look at 13. Circle T for true and F for false.**

1 Artists sometimes use chewing gum.   T   F

2 Galleries show art to the public.   T   F

3 Photographers design websites.   T   F

4 A good photographer always carries a camera.   T   F

5 Fashion designers design cars.   T   F

15 Look at 13. Match to make phrases from the text.

1 chewing
2 plastic
3 art
4 water
5 wild
6 fashion
7 photo

a animals
b gum
c gallery
d shoot
e show
f bag
g color

16 Complete the crossword. Use the clues and the words from the box.

designer   gallery   landscapes   photographer   sketch   upload

Down ↓

1 When Susie has an idea she draws a ?.

4 Jake shows his paintings in an art ?.

Across →

2 Jake likes painting the mountains. He paints ?.

3 A ? takes pictures of people and places.

5 I ? my pictures to the computer.

6 Susie loves drawing clothes. She's a fashion ?.

THINK BIG

When fashion designers see people wearing their clothes, they feel happy. When do you feel happy?

When I _____, I feel happy.

17 **Read and write.**

> am   is   live   study   take   wants   work   works

I ¹ _____ a scientist, and I ² _____ at a laboratory at the college. I usually work from 9 a.m. to 5 or 6 p.m., but sometimes I stay late and I ³ _____. My friend ⁴ _____ a nurse and ⁵ _____ at the local hospital. Sometimes he also stays late. I want to ⁶ _____ on a farm one day. My friend likes farms, too. He ⁷ _____ to ⁸ _____ care of animals instead of people!

18 **Choose the correct word and ✓.**

1 I
- ☐ study   at night.
- ☐ studies

2 We
- ☐ live   on a farm.
- ☐ lives

3 She
- ☐ work   at a hospital.
- ☐ works

4 He
- ☐ travel   all over the world.
- ☐ travels

5 They
- ☐ stay   at Park Hotel.
- ☐ stays

6 They
- ☐ love   animals.
- ☐ loves

Grammar

19 **Look and write. What do they do?**

1 He's a _____   **2** _____   **3** _____

4 _____   **5** _____   **6** _____

20 **Write questions and answers.**

1 **A:** _____ (he/work/hospital)

     B: _____. _____ fire station.

2 **A:** _____ (she/work/police station)

     B: _____. _____ school.

3 **A:** _____ (you/eat/restaurant)

     B: _____. _____ home.

4 **A:** _____ (Dad/play soccer/Saturday)

     B: _____. _____ Friday.

5 **A:** _____ (they/live/Mexico City)

     B: _____. _____ Buenos Aires.

21 **Read. Find the three countries.**

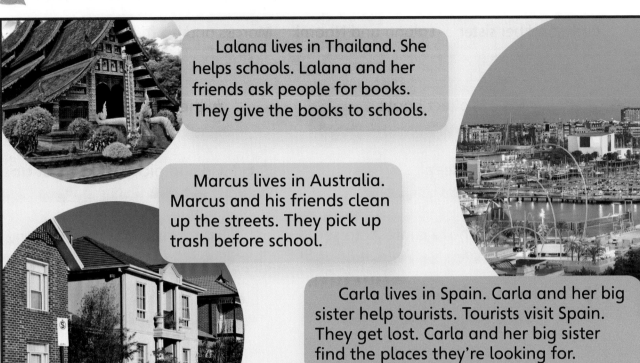

Lalana lives in Thailand. She helps schools. Lalana and her friends ask people for books. They give the books to schools.

Marcus lives in Australia. Marcus and his friends clean up the streets. They pick up trash before school.

Carla lives in Spain. Carla and her big sister help tourists. Tourists visit Spain. They get lost. Carla and her big sister find the places they're looking for.

22 **Listen, read, and complete. Use the words from the box.**

36

| clean collect community donate helping lost trash world |

1   A lot of people say they want to make the ¹ _____ a better place. Many don't do anything, but many do lots of useful and helpful things. Start with where you live. When you do good things to help your ² _____, you help the world, too.

2   In Chiang Mai, Thailand, many schools don't have money to buy books. Lalana and Naomi help by asking people to ³ _____ books. They ⁴ _____ the books and take them to schools in their city. Now the schools have books.

3   In Melbourne, Australia, Marcus sees ⁵ _____ on the roads when he walks to school. So he and his friends pick up the trash. They have contests to see who can collect the most. They keep the streets ⁶ _____ and it's fun.

4   In Barcelona, Spain, Carla helps tourists when they get ⁷ _____. She loves her city and she likes ⁸ _____ people. She and her sister help tourists on weekends.

23 **Look at 22. Read and match. Then write.**

Carla and her sister   Lalana and Naomi   Marcus and his friends

1 _____ collect books

a the streets clean.

2 _____ keep

b who can pick up the most trash.

3 _____ have contests to see

c tourists on weekends.

4 _____ help

d and take them to schools.

24 **Read and write.**

about   for   in   to   with

1 To make the world a better place, start _____ where you live.

2 Let's do something _____ it!

3 They have better books, thanks _____ Lalana and Naomi.

4 We help tourists look _____ places to visit.

5 He picks up trash _____ the streets.

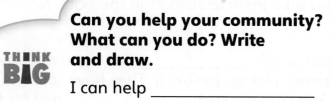

THINK BIG

Can you help your community? What can you do? Write and draw.

I can help _____

_____

_____

_____

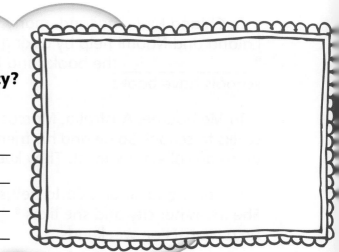

25 **Circle the subjects and underline the verbs.**

Steve and Mohammed are friends. They work at a laboratory. They play basketball and watch TV on a Saturday.

26 **Rachel and Kate are sisters. Read and complete.**

Rachel

I am a police officer.

I dance.

I sing.

I live on a farm.

Kate

I am a teacher.

I dance.

I play the piano.

I live in a city.

1 _____ and _____ are sisters.

2 _____ and _____ dance.

3 _____ dances and sings.

4 _____ dances and plays the piano.

5 _____ lives in a city.

6 _____ lives on a farm.

27 **Write about you.**

I _____ and _____ in the evening.

My friend and I _____ after school.

28 **Read and circle sm, st, sk, and sp.**

smile

game

spoon

storm

space

smart

ski   star

skate

note

29 **Underline the words with sm, st, sk, and sp. Then read aloud.**

1 There are small stars in space.

2 We skate and ski in the winter.

30 **Connect the letters. Then write.**

1 sm   oon   **a** _ _ _ _ _
2 sp   ar   **b** _ _ _ _
3 st   i   **c** _ _ _
4 sk   ile   **d** _ _ _ _ _

41
31 **Listen and write.**

¹ _____ and look.
Look at the ² _____,
The stars in ³ _____,
And ⁴ _____!

32 **Look and complete. Then answer.**

1 What _____ your sister do?

☐ **a** She's a teacher.
☐ **b** She's a police officer.

2 What _____ your mom _____?

☐ **a** She's a waiter.
☐ **b** She's a scientist.

3 What _____ your brothers do?

☐ **a** They're firefighters.
☐ **b** They're students.

4 What _____ your cousins _____?

☐ **a** They're nurses.
☐ **b** They're farmers.

33 **Read and match.**

1 I like dancing. When I

2 When they take a picture, they

3 When she has an idea,

4 When he sees a beautiful landscape,

5 I get ideas when

a she draws a sketch.

b dance, I feel happy.

c he paints it.

d I go to an art gallery.

e upload it to a computer.

unit 3

Working Hard!

1 Follow and write. Use the words from the box.

bed	dishes	dog	fish
piano	room	test	trash

1 clean — my
2 do — the
3 feed — the
4 make — my
5 practice — the
6 study — for — a
7 take — out — the
8 walk — the

_____
_____
_____
_____
_____
_____
_____
_____

46
2 Listen. What things do they do? Match. Then write.

1 Tara _____
_____.

2 Dave _____
_____.

3 Christy _____
_____.

4 Matt _____
_____.

 **a**

 **b**

 **c**

 **d**

3 **Listen and circle.**

Different Twins

My name's Matt,
And my name's Mike.
We want to talk to you.
I do my chores,
And I do, too.
But we are not alike.

**Mike and Matt, Matt and Mike.
These two twins are not alike.**

I'm Matt,
I always **take out the trash / clean my room.**
I do my chores each day.
I sometimes **do the dishes / study for a test,**
And then we go and play.

Chorus

I'm Mike,
I always **clean my room / make my bed.**
I do my chores each day.
I sometimes **feed the fish / walk the dog,**
And then we go and play.

Chorus

4 **What chores do you do? Write four sentences.**

_____

_____

_____

_____

5 **Read. Then number in order.**

I Have a Lot to Do

Amy is thinking. She's making a list. She has to do a lot of things before school. She has to eat breakfast. She has to brush her teeth. Then she has to feed her fish, clean her room, and study for her math test. Amy goes to school at 7:50. Her alarm clock says 7:05. Mom says "It's 7:45." Amy's clock isn't working! She has to get a new alarm clock.

_____ She has to study for her math test.

_____ She has to feed the fish.

_____ She has to brush her teeth.

_____ Amy has to eat breakfast.

_____ She has to get a new alarm clock.

_____ She has to clean her room.

6 **Write. What do you have to do before school?**

I have to _____ before school.

Think and write for you.

THINK BIG

1 I have to _____ before I go to bed.

2 I have to _____ before I go to bed.

3 I have to _____ before I go to bed.

4 I have to _____ before I go to bed.

52

7 Listen and stick.

Monday	Tuesday	Wednesday	Thursday	Friday

8 Read and circle the correct words.

1 **A:** What **do / does** Nancy have to do after school?

B: She **have to / has to** practice the piano.

2 **A:** What **do / does** we have to do this evening?

B: We **have to / has to** study for our test tomorrow.

3 **A:** What **do / does** you have to do every morning?

B: I **have to / has to** make my bed.

9 What do they have to do? Look and write.

Kate and Ted

Jane

Jim and Mike

1 Kate: _____

2 Ted: _____

3 Jane: _____

4 Jim and Mike: _____

Language in Action

10 **Look and match.**

1 always

	Sun	Mon	Tue	Wed	Thurs	Fri	Sat
a							

2 usually

	Sun	Mon	Tue	Wed	Thurs	Fri	Sat
b							

3 sometimes

	Sun	Mon	Tue	Wed	Thurs	Fri	Sat
c							

4 never

	Sun	Mon	Tue	Wed	Thurs	Fri	Sat
d							

11 **Complete with always, usually, sometimes, or never.**

1 I _____ feed the fish.

2 I _____ study for tests.

3 I _____ take out the trash.

4 I _____ do the dishes.

	M	T	W	T	F
feed the fish	✔		✔		✔
study for a test				✔	✔
take out the trash					
do the dishes	✔	✔	✔	✔	✔

12 **Complete for you. Use the verbs from the box.**

clean   do   make   practice   study   take

1 I usually _____.

2 I sometimes _____.

3 I never _____.

4 I always _____.

13 **Read and match.**

1	walk the	**a**	plants
2	clean the	**b**	breakfast
3	take out the	**c**	dog
4	water the	**d**	room
5	wash	**e**	trash
6	make	**f**	the car

55

14 **Listen, read, and write. Then check your answers in 13.**

buy   cash   earn   housework   pocket   safe   save

1   As children, we don't have money. Our parents usually ¹ _____ the things we need. They sometimes give us some ² _____ money, too. But soon, we want to buy things which cost more money, and we need to find extra cash.

2   There's always a lot to do around the house. Maybe you can ask your parents to give you some money for helping with the ³ _____? Or maybe you can earn ⁴ _____ by cleaning your room, taking out the trash, making breakfast, or doing the dishes.

3   You can also ⁵ _____ money by helping friends and neighbors. For example you can help in the yard or water the plants in the house. You can walk the dog or wash the car, too. Of course, you have to make sure you're ⁶ _____. Don't work for strangers. Always tell your parents where you are, and ask to know that it's ok.

4   Then, buy some nice things but try to ⁷ _____ a little bit of the money you make every time. This way you always have extra cash.

15 Look at 14. Circle **T** for true and **F** for false.

1 Parents usually buy children the things they need. **T   F**

2 There's never a lot to do around the house. **T   F**

3 Washing a dog is a good way to earn cash. **T   F**

4 We should never work for strangers. **T   F**

5 Saving some money is a bad idea. **T   F**

16 Put the words in order.

1 I | dog. | when | money | the | earn | walk | I

_____

2 when | cents | earns | dishes. | Nadia | fifty | she | the | does

_____

3 twice | cooked | week. | Alex | this | dinner

_____

4 morning | made | week. | this | every | bed | his | Erol

_____

5 earned | her | $4.50. | cleaned | and | room | Rosa

_____

I earn two dollars each time I clean my room. I clean it twice a week. How much pocket money do I earn?

THINK BIG Read and ✓.

$2 x 1 = $2 ☐ $2 x 2 = $4 ☐ $1 x 3 = $3 ☐

**Is it better to spend or save pocket money? Why?
How much of your pocket money should you save?**

17 **Look at the chart. Circle T for true and F for false.**

	watch movies	have parties	spend time at home	clean up	walk the dog
Mike	***	***	**	*	***
Angela	****	***	***	*	****

**** love   *** like   ** not like   * hate

1   Mike likes cleaning up.   T   F

2   Mike loves walking the dog.   T   F

3   Angela likes spending time at home.   T   F

4   Mike loves having parties.   T   F

5   Angela loves watching movies.   T   F

6   Angela hates cleaning up.   T   F

18 **Look at 17. Write sentences.**

1   Angela/walk the dog

_____

2   Mike/watch movies

_____

3   Mike/spend time at home

_____

4   Angela/clean up

_____

5   Mike and Angela/have parties

_____

Grammar

19 **Write questions with like, love, and hate.**

1 he/like/walk the dog?

_____

2 you/love/play soccer?

_____

3 she/hate/do the dishes?

_____

4 they/hate/clean/their rooms?

_____

5 your cat/like/play/with a ball?

_____

20 **Write the -ing form.**

1 swim	_____	**2** spend	_____
3 sit	_____	**4** give	_____
5 feed	_____	**6** let	_____
7 take	_____	**8** study	_____

21 **Answer the questions about you. Use like, love, and hate.**

1 Do you like watching action movies?

Yes, I do. I love watching action movies.

No, I don't like/hate watching action movies. I love watching comedies.

2 Do you like doing homework?

_____

_____

3 Do you like washing the dishes?

_____

_____

4 Do you like playing soccer?

_____

_____

22 **Read and match.**

a

1 Leah lives in Alaska. She has to shovel snow before school.

b

2 Ivan lives on a farm. He has to feed the goats before school.

3 Chen Wei's mom has a noodle restaurant. She has to help her mother make noodles.

c

58

23 **Listen, read, and write.**

| care | chores | clear | helps | keep | makes | task | tiring |

1   Around the world, many children help their parents with ¹ _____. Some also do chores as part of life in a family business. Difficult tasks always become easy when you have help.

2   There's usually a lot of snow on the roads and the sidewalks in Alaska. Everyone has to shovel snow to ² _____ their entrances ³ _____. Leah shovels snow before she goes to school every day. She likes her ⁴ _____.

3   Ivan lives in France on a farm. He gets milk from the goats on his farm to make goat's cheese, and then he sells it. He ⁵ _____ his father take ⁶ _____ of the goats. Every morning, he has to get up early to feed them. He goes to school after his work on the farm.

4   Chen Wei's mother ⁷ _____ the best noodles in Singapore. Everyone knows her and wants her noodles. People come from all over the country to try them. It's ⁸ _____ work in the kitchen, so after she does her homework, Chen Wei helps her mother. She also loves eating them!

24 **Look at 23. Read and circle.**

1 There is a lot of **noodles / snow** in Alaska.

2 People use **shovels / spoons** to clear it.

3 Ivan gets up **late / early** every day to work on the **road / farm**.

4 Chen Wei's mother makes the best noodles in **Singapore / China**. Chen Wei loves **selling / eating** them!

25 **Put the words in order.**

1 | lot | snow. | There | a | is | of |

_____

2 | clear | the | shovels | She | entrance. | snow | to |

_____

3 | the | They | make | cheese | farm. | on | goat |

_____

4 | get | every | has | to | early | morning. | up | He |

_____

5 | noodles | Making | work. | is | tiring |

_____

6 | her | Chen Wei | homework | mother. | she | before | helps | her | does |

_____

Put a ✓ to the chores.

THINK BIG

go to a party ☐   clean the kitchen ☐

play in the yard ☐   feed the fish ☐

walk the dog ☐   watch television ☐

make your bed ☐   listen to music ☐

26 **Read. Then ✗ the words we don't write in capitals.**

> Use **capital letters** for most words in titles.
> **I** H**ave a** L**ot to** D**o!**
>
> But always use capital letters for the first word in a title.
> **A** Day at the Park with Grandma

and, but, or, a, an, the ☐

grandpa, mom, brother ☐

at, for, in, on, to, with ☐

big, good ☐

help, walk, eat ☐

Taking Care of a Big Dog

Good Things to Eat

My Brother and I

27 **Circle the title with the correct capitals.**

1 A big blue balloon
   a Big Blue Balloon
   A Big Blue Balloon

2 The Chef and the Waiter
   the Chef and the Waiter
   The Chef And The Waiter

3 Harry Needs a Helping Hand
   Harry needs a Helping Hand
   Harry Needs A Helping Hand

4 Dinner At Grandpa's House
   Dinner at Grandpa's House
   Dinner at grandpa's house

28 **Write the correct title. Use capital letters.**

1 _____

uncle Joe's dream
penguin trouble at the zoo
a surprise for grandma

2 _____

3 _____

29 **Read and circle ay and oy.**

bike

say

day

May

boy

toy

stop

joy

30 **Underline the words with ay and oy. Then read aloud.**

1 On Sundays, we play all day with our toys.

2 I'm reading the story of a boy named Roy.

31 **Connect the letters. Then write.**

1 d   oy   **a** _ _ _

2 t   ay   **b** _ _ _

63
32 **Listen and write.**

What do we ¹_____?

It's May, it's ²_____,

It's a nice ³_____.

Come on, girls!

Come on, ⁴_____!

Bring your ⁵_____.

33 **Look, read, and ✓.**

I clean my room three times a week. I get fifty cents each time. How much pocket money do I earn?

I take out the trash four times a week. I get one dollar each time. How much pocket money do I earn?

50c x 2 = $1 ☐
$3 x 1= $3 ☐
50c x 3 = $1.50 ☐

$1 x 3= $3 ☐
$1 x 4= $4 ☐
50c x 3 = $1.50 ☐

34 **Look. Write T for true and F for false.**

Alicia's Chores	Monday	Tuesday	Wednesday	Thursday	Friday
make the bed	✓	✓	✓	✓	✓
do the dishes	✓		✓		
feed the fish	✓	✓	✓	✓	
take out the trash					

1 Alicia always makes the bed. _____

2 Alicia never does the dishes. _____

3 Alicia usually feeds the fish. _____

4 Alicia sometimes takes out the trash. _____

35 **Look and write about Josh and Adam. Use has to and have to.**

	Josh	Adam
walk the dog	✓	✓
practice the piano	✓	
study for a test	✓	✓
clean his room		✓

1 Josh and Adam _____

_____ dog.

2 _____

_____ piano.

3 _____ test.

4 _____ room.

Sue's Busy Day

1 Choose one path. Draw the path. Learn about Sue's busy day.

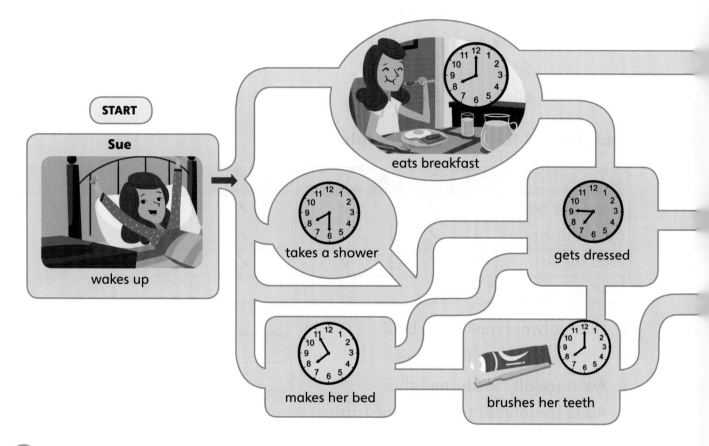

START

Sue

wakes up

eats breakfast

takes a shower

gets dressed

makes her bed

brushes her teeth

2 Look at your path in 1. Guess and write.

1 What time does Sue wake up? She wakes up at _____.

2 What does Sue do? She's a _____.

3 Look at your path in 1. Write five sentences about Sue's day.

1 _____

2 _____

3 _____

4 _____

5 _____

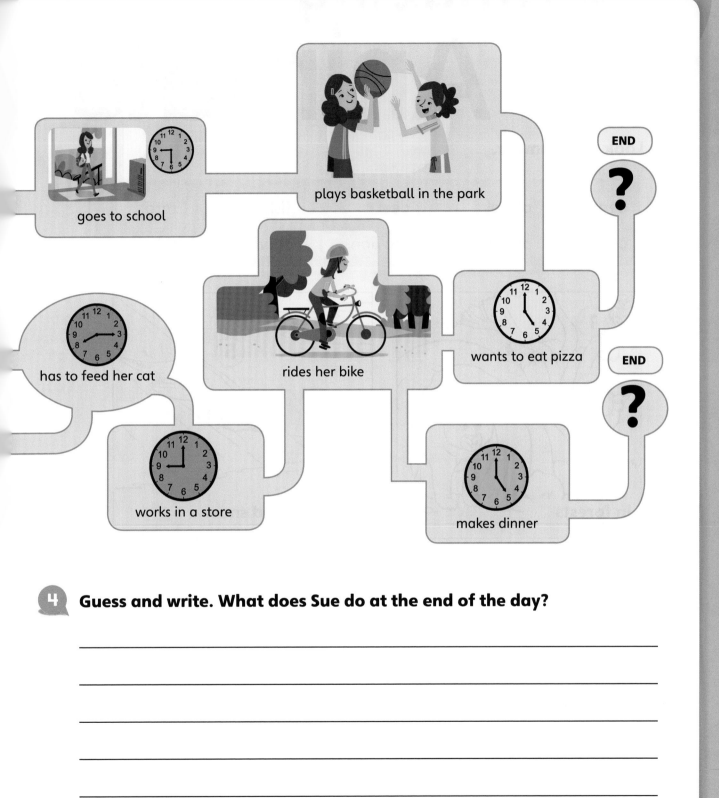

goes to school

plays basketball in the park

END

?

has to feed her cat

rides her bike

wants to eat pizza

END

?

works in a store

makes dinner

4 **Guess and write. What does Sue do at the end of the day?**

_____

_____

_____

_____

_____

_____

Amazing Animals

1 **Look and number.**

bear ☐ camel ☐ deer ☐ fish ☐ lizard ☐

owl ☐ penguin ☐ sea lion ☐ shark ☐ snake ☐

in forests

in the ice and snow

in deserts

in oceans

2 **Write.**

My favorite animals are _____.

They _____.

3 Listen and write. Then number. Underline the places.

a

b

Animals Are Amazing!

Animals are amazing!
We see them far and near.
Some live in forests

Like ¹ _____, ² _____,
and ³ _____.

Some live in deserts

Like ⁴ _____
and some ⁵ _____.

Some live in water,
In oceans, seas, and lakes.

**Amazing, amazing animals
What can animals do?
They can fly, they can swim, they can jump!
We share the earth with you!**

c

d

e

4 Answer the questions.

1 Where do bears live?

_____

2 Where do fish live?

_____

3 Where do toucans live?

_____

4 Where do camels live?

_____

5 **Read. Then write can or can't.**

At the Zoo

Luke and Amy are at the zoo. They watch a sea lion show. The sea lion can clap to music. It can't sing very well so Luke covers his ears. The sea lion can balance a ball. It can do lots of tricks. Luke and Amy go to the parrot show. The parrot can ride a bike. It can say its name. It can talk! The parrot can't stop talking.

1 The sea lion _____ clap to music.

2 The sea lion _____ sing well.

3 The sea lion _____ do tricks.

4 The parrot _____ ride a bike.

5 The parrot _____ say its name.

6 The parrot _____ stop talking.

6 **Write about what you can do.**

> balance a ball on your nose   clap to music   ride a bike   sing well

I can _____.

I can't _____.

THINK BIG

> do tricks   fly
> jump   swim
> talk   walk

Sea lions can _____.

They can't _____.

Parrots _____.

_____

74
7 **Listen and stick. Then number.**

a  b c  d

☐   ☐   ☐   ☐

8 **Look and complete the sentences. Use can or can't.**

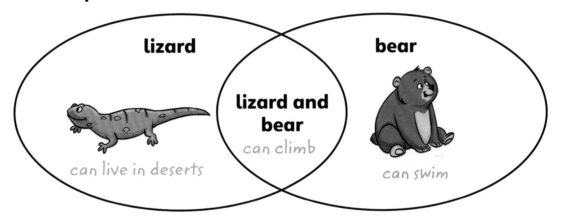

lizard   lizard and bear   bear
can live in deserts   can climb   can swim

1 Lizards and bears _____.

2 Lizards _____ but bears _____.

3 Bears _____ but lizards _____.

9 **Read and circle.**

1 Can **a camel / camels** live in deserts?
   Yes, it can.

2 Can **a lizard / lizards** climb? Yes, they can.

3 Can **bears / a bear** fly? No, they can't.

4 Can **a shark / sharks** walk? No, it can't.

10 **Answer the questions.**

1 Can a bear climb?

_____

2 Can penguins fly?

_____

3 Can a shark sing?

_____

4 Can lizards talk?

_____

5 Can sea lions do tricks?

_____

11 **Look and complete. Use the words from the box.**

can   can't   fly   swim   they

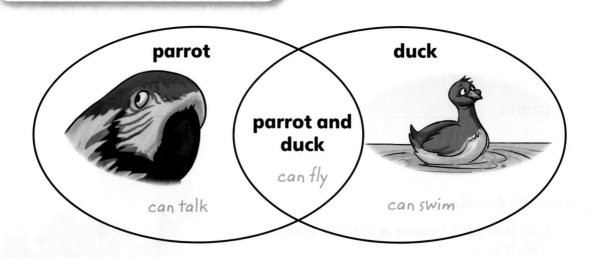

parrot

parrot and duck

can fly

duck

can talk

can swim

Parrots and ducks can ¹_____. Parrots ²_____ talk
but ³_____ can't swim. Ducks can ⁴_____ but they
⁵_____ talk.

12 **Look and write.**

> chameleon   gray tree frog   polar bear   stonefish

1 _____

2 _____

3 _____

4 _____

77

13 **Read and circle. Then listen and check.**

1   The polar bear lives on the ice and ¹ **snow / rocks** of the polar regions. Everywhere is white, so its white fur blends in with its surroundings. Polar bears can run ² **fast / slowly**, and they can swim, too, which makes them great hunters in the ocean as well as on the ice and snow.

2   In rain forests and in deserts, the ³ **shape / color** of the surroundings isn't always the same. The chameleon's camouflage is very smart because it can change its color to ⁴ **blend in / hunt fish**. When it's in a ⁵ **tree / desert**, it's green. When it's on a rock, it's brown or gray.

3   Stonefish live in the ocean. They like to eat fish, so they sit on the bottom of the ⁶ **ocean / tree** and wait. They look like stones, so the fish can't see them. If a fish touches it, the stonefish stings it and kills it. Then it eats the fish.

4   In the forests of North America, there are gray tree frogs. Birds and ⁷ **polar bears / snakes** like to eat them, but they look like tree branches! Their camouflage helps them ⁸ **hunt / hide**.

14 **Read and match.**

1 A polar bear

2 A chameleon

3 A stonefish

4 A gray tree frog

a waits at the bottom of the ocean, and kills fish with its sting.

b can camouflage by changing its color.

c can hide from danger because it loo~~ like branches in the forest.

d is difficult to see because all its fur is white.

15 **Look at 13. Circle T for true and F for false.**

1 The polar bear changes the color of its fur to blend in.   T   F

2 Polar bears are great hunters.   T   F

3 The chameleon changes the color of its surroundings.   T   F

4 The stonefish can eat stones.   T   F

5 Gray tree frogs look like snakes.   T   F

6 Gray tree frogs can live in trees.   T   F

THINK BIG

Complete and color.

1 A chameleon on a brown rock is _____.

2 A chameleon on a green branch is _____.

16 **Complete the table.**

quiet	quietly
slow	1 _____
easy	easily
2 _____	carefully
good	3 _____
fast	fast
hard	4 _____
far	5 _____
6 _____	badly

17 **Read and ✓ the correct sentences.**

1 Camels can walk very far. ☐

2 Kangaroos jump very well. ☐

3 A crocodile's skin is very hardly. ☐

4 Monkeys can climb good. ☐

5 Sea lions are good swimmers. ☐

6 This bird sings so beautiful. ☐

7 Bats listen carefully. ☐

8 Polar bears run very fastly. ☐

18 **Look at 17. Correct the wrong sentences.**

1 _____

2 _____

3 _____

4 _____

Grammar

19 **Read and circle.**

1 My parrot is so **noisy / noisily**.

Our dog eats **noisy / noisily**.

2 You have to be **quiet / quietly** in the library.

Please read **quiet / quietly**!

3 Snakes move **quick / quickly** to catch food.

It's a **quick / quickly** walk to the pet store.

4 This computer is very **slow / slowly**.

The camel walked **slow / slowly** across the hot desert.

5 The English test is **easy / easily**.

I can **easy / easily** do my homework.

6 She speaks English very **good / well**.

The new Captain America movie is very **good / well**.

7 Look at this! I draw very **bad / badly**!

Look at this! It's a very **bad / badly** drawing!

20 **Read and write.**

> carefully   far   good   hard   quietly   well

1 The shopping mall isn't very _____.

2 If you look _____, you'll see the deer behind the tree.

3 You have to speak _____ in the library.

4 Speak up! I can't hear you very _____.

5 This movie is very _____.

6 I have to study _____ for this test.

21 **Look and write.**

canary   cat   dog   lizard   snake

1 _____

2 _____

3 _____

4 _____

5 _____

22 **Read and write. Use your answers in 21. Then listen and check.**

1   Pets are good company and relax us when we play with them. They can also be helpful. When we walk our [1] _____, we stay in shape. They can keep us safe, too, and cats keep mice and the insects away.

2   In China, people like to have a [2] _____ as a pet, and the Chinese believe that they bring good luck to a home. In the U.S.A., there are about 93 million of them!

3   Birds are popular pets, too. In Mexico, the parakeet is a favorite bird. Parakeets can talk and they like playing! In Italy, the [3] _____ is a popular pet bird. These birds sing beautifully!

4   There are dangerous pets, too. You can have a tarantula! When they bite, it's very painful, but they're usually quiet and don't bite. Some people have a pet [4] _____ or alligator, so the owner has to be very careful. There are millions of owners of pet reptiles around the world. A gecko, an iguana or a [5] _____ can be interesting to have. They're exotic and not dangerous.

5   We all like different pets for different reasons. The important thing is to take care of your pet and to love it as part of your family.

23 **Look at 22. Read and match.**

1 Pets are good to have because

2 Cats are popular in China because

3 The canary is a popular bird because

4 Be careful with your tarantula because

5 A lizard can be a good pet because

a it's exotic and interesting but not dangerous.

b it sings beautifully.

c it might give you a painful bite.

d they relax us and can be helpful.

e people believe they bring good luck.

24 **Put the words in order.**

1 | all | different | like | pets. | We |

_____

2 | have | dangerous | Some | people | pets. |

_____

3 | have to | You | pet. | love and | your | take care of |

_____

4 | insects | Cats | our houses. | keep | from | mice and | away |

_____

5 | U.S.A. | pet cats | the | about | 93 million | in | are | There |

_____

Read and write about you.

THINK BIG

My name is _____. I live in _____.

_____ are popular pets here. They can

_____ and _____. They can't

_____ or _____.

25 **Read. Circle the best topic sentence for the main idea.**

1 Main idea: Polar bears are my favorite animal.

  a Polar bears live in cold places.

  b Some days are cold in the winter.

  c I like polar bears.

2 Main idea: It's important to take care of pets.

  a I want a pet parakeet.

  b I feed my cat every day.

  c People all over the world have pets.

3 Main idea: Some animals can change color.

  a Some animals can look like different things.

  b Some animals are not good pets.

  c Some animals can do tricks.

4 Main idea: Zoos are great places.

  a A parrot can talk.

  b I always have fun at the zoo.

  c Dogs are fun pets.

26 **Write a topic sentence for the following titles.**

1 My Favorite Animal

_____

2 My Favorite Time of Day

_____

3 An Unusual Job

_____

27 **Read and circle ea, oi, and oe.**

eat   Spain   boil

        bean   meat

    toe   oil   joy

28 **Underline the words with ea, oi, and oe. Then read aloud.**

1 Joe likes boiled beans with oil.

2 I eat meat and drink tea.

29 **Connect the letters. Then write.**

1 p   oil   **a** _ _ _ _

2 b   oe   **b** _ _ _

3 t   each   **c** _ _ _ _ _

86

30 **Listen and write.**

So, Joe, boil the ¹ _____,
Add the ² _____,
Add the ³ _____.
Eat the ⁴ _____,
Eat the meat,
Eat the ⁵ _____,
And drink the ⁶ _____.

31 **Read and answer.**

1 Can snakes eat sharks? _____

2 Can a bear climb? _____

3 Can a lizard sing? _____

4 Can parrots talk? _____

32 **Think about the animals you know. Complete the chart.**

These animals can swim.	These animals can fly.	These animals can climb trees.
1	1	1
2	2	2
3	3	3
4	4	4

33 **Match the questions and answers.**

1 What can toucans do?

2 What can you do?

3 Can an owl jump?

4 Can a shark swim?

5 What can a parrot do?

6 Can deer jump and run?

a Yes, it can.

b They can fly.

c Yes, they can.

d No, it can't, but it can fly.

e I can swim, run, and talk.

f It can fly, but it can't swim.

34 **Correct the sentences.**

1 Sea lions can swim good. _____

2 Canaries sing beautiful. _____

3 Sea lions sing bad. _____

4 A chameleon can change color easy. _____

Wonderful Weather!

1 **Match.**

1

2

3

4

5

6

 a It's hot and sunny.

 b It's windy.

 c It's cool and cloudy.

 d It's cold and snowy.

 e It's rainy.

 f It's warm.

2 **What's the weather like today?**

It's _____.

It isn't _____.

3 Listen and circle the five incorrect words. Then listen and write.

Cool Weekend!

What's the weather like today?
Rainy, windy, hot, or cold?

On Sunday, it was rainy,
It was very hot, too.
I was nice and cool in my winter coat,
Outside the sky wasn't blue!

Now it's Tuesday. It's sunny.
Great! I can go out and play.
Oh, no! I have to go to school.
Never mind! The weekend was cold!

Chorus (x2)

1 _____

2 _____

3 _____

4 _____

5 _____

4 Look at 1. Complete the sentences. Use words from the box.

coat   scarf   shorts   sunglasses   T-shirt

1 On hot and sunny days, Jim wears _____.

2 On warm days, Iris wears a _____.

3 On cloudy and cool days, Dan wears a _____.

4 On warm rainy days, Maria wears _____ and boots.

5 On cold and snowy days, Joe wears a _____.

5 What was the weather like yesterday? Draw and write.

It was _____. It wasn't _____.

6 Read and ✓.

Amy is Ready!

Amy is going on a hike. It was rainy yesterday. Amy's mom doesn't want her to get wet today, so Amy gets a raincoat and an umbrella. It was cold and windy yesterday. Amy's mom doesn't want her to get cold, so she gets her sweater, her hat, and gloves. It's sunny today. Amy's mom gives her sunscreen and sunglasses. Now Amy's ready!

1 It was rainy yesterday. Amy gets

☐ sunglasses. ☐ an umbrella. ☐ a sweater. ☐ a raincoat.

2 It was cold and windy yesterday. Amy gets

☐ a sweater. ☐ sandals. ☐ shorts. ☐ gloves.

3 It's warm and sunny now. Amy's mom gives her

☐ boots. ☐ a coat. ☐ sunscreen. ☐ sunglasses.

cloudy   cold   cool   hot   rainy   snowy

7 Read and write.

1 What is the weather like today? It's _____.

2 What was the weather like yesterday? It was _____.

THINK BIG   Draw and write.

HOT

COLD

I wear _____ on sunny days.

I wear _____ on cold days.

95
8 **Listen and stick.**

San Francisco	
Yesterday	Today

Puerto Rico	
Yesterday	Today

9 **What was the weather like? Match and write.**

1   On Monday, _____.

2   _____

3   _____

4   _____

5   _____

10 Read and look. Circle **T** for true and **F** for false.

Yesterday	Today

1 Yesterday, the weather was cool.	T	F
2 It wasn't windy yesterday.	T	F
3 It's cloudy today.	T	F
4 It's cold today.	T	F
5 It was sunny yesterday.	T	F
6 It's cool and sunny today.	T	F

11 Look at **10**. Write the answers.

1 What was the weather like yesterday? _____

2 What is the weather like today? _____

12 Write about you.

1 What was the weather like yesterday? _____

13 Read and make sentences.

1 I / ✗ / hot / yesterday

_____

2 We / ✗ / cool / last weekend

_____

3 It / ✓ / sunny / now

_____

4 It / ✗ / windy / today

_____

14 **What's the weather like? Look and write.**

1 _____

2 _____

3 _____

4 _____

5 _____

97

15 **Read and write. Then listen and check your answers.**

climate   extreme   moon   opposite   seasons   temperature

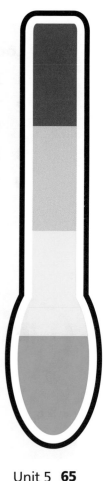

1   The weather in a place is called the ¹ _____. Different places on the planet have different climates, and these change with the ² _____. In some places, like Southern Europe, winters are mild, and it's often rainy with not much snow. But in other places, the climate is extreme – the weather is very hot, very cold, or there's a lot of rain.

2   In the Lut Desert in Iran, for example, it's very hot and dry. The ³ _____ can reach 70 degrees Celsius. This is why there's no life there in some parts – and no tourists! However, a lot of tourists visit the Atacama Desert in Chile. It's also dry there, but temperatures are milder. Atacama looks like the surface of the ⁴ _____ – it almost never rains there. On the other hand, it rains almost every day in Lloró, Colombia. Trees grow quickly there because it's so wet.

3   If you like very cold temperatures, you can visit a place like Oymyakon, Russia. It's the ⁵ _____ of a place like Lut Desert. The winters there are ⁶ _____, with temperatures as low as -70 degrees Celsius. There's a lot of snow and ice, and schools only close if the temperature is below -52 degrees Celsius!

16 Look at **15** and match.

1 Atacama Desert, Chile

2 Oymyakon, Russia

3 Lloró, Colombia

4 Lut Desert, Iran

a

b

c

d

17 Look at **15**. Read and match.

1 Not many people go to the Lut Desert.   a because of the cold climate.
2 The Atacama desert is very dry   b As a result, the trees grow quickly.
3 It rains a lot in Lloró, Colombia.   c As a result, it's a quiet place.
4 Not many people live in Oymyakon   d because it never rains.

18 Look at **15**. Read and write.

1 It snows a lot in _____, _____.
2 The _____ Desert in _____ is dry and looks like the moon.
3 It's very wet in _____, _____.
4 It's too hot to live in the _____ _____, Iran.

Find the one that doesn't belong.

1 Lloró   2 Atacama Desert
3 Lut Desert   4 Oymyakon, Russia

The one that doesn't belong is _____

because _____.

19 **Look and write. Use was or wasn't.**

M	T	W	Th	F

1 Last Monday, it _____ sunny.

2 Last Tuesday, it _____ rainy.

3 Last Wednesday, it _____ cloudy.

4 Last Thursday, it _____ windy.

5 Last Friday, it _____ snowy.

20 **Read and circle.**

1   There **was** / **were** a lot of rain.

2   There **was** / **were** boats on the river.

3   There **was** / **were** sharks in the water.

4   There **was** / **were** children in the park.

5   There **was** / **were** a kite in the sky.

6   There **was** / **were** a snowman in the road!

21 **Look at 20. Make negative sentences.**

1 _____

2 _____

3 _____

4 _____

5 _____

6 _____

22 **Read and write. Use was, were, or weren't.**

Danny and Leo ¹ _____ lost in the forest and
it ² _____ late. Then there ³ _____
a noise. ⁴ _____ it an owl? ⁵ _____
there bears here? The boys ⁶ _____ sure. Leo
⁷ _____ scared. He ⁸ _____ cold,
and he ⁹ _____ hungry. "Look!" said Danny.
There ¹⁰ _____ a house. The lights
¹¹ _____ on. "Come on!" he said. There
¹² _____ nice people in the house. Danny and
Leo ¹³ _____ happy.

23 **Read the answers and write questions.**

1 He was in New York last year.
Where _____?

2 She was in bed at 9 p.m. last night.
When _____?

3 Her aunt was in the hospital.
Where _____?

4 They were at our house last weekend.
When _____?

5 John was with Eric's parents.
Who _____?

6 Mary and Anna were at the stores this morning.
Where _____?

7 They were at work at 7 a.m. yesterday morning.
What time _____?

99

24 **Read and circle. Then listen and check your answers.**

1   **¹ Sports / exams** are fun for children everywhere. Baseball and basketball are very popular in the U.S.A. Cricket and field hockey are favorite sports in India and England. Soccer is popular everywhere. Kids love to be **² active / asleep**.

2   If the **³ weather / television** is bad, you can still have **⁴ fun / chores**. When it's windy, you can fly a kite. In some Asian countries, like Japan, children love flying kites. Some like to make their own kites, and you can try this, too! Just look on the Internet for ideas.

3   For much of the year, parts of Africa are very dry. When lots of **⁵ rain / weather** comes, the lakes and rivers fill up, and children can go swimming and **⁶ play / work** in the water.

4   Snow is fun, too, of course. You can go **⁷ skiing / swimming** or sledding, or you can make **⁸ dinner / snowmen**. You can have snowball fights as well. In places with a lot of snow, such as Canada and Alaska, some kids go dog sledding. Dogs pull sleds in the snow, and the kids ride on them.

5   So, when the weather is bad, don't stay **⁹ at school / inside**. Put on the right clothes or get an umbrella and go **¹⁰ to bed / outside**!

25 **Which paragraph? Look at 24 and match paragraphs 1–5 to pictures a–e.**

a

b

c

d

e

26 **Read and match.**

1 Some children fly kites   **a** on rainy days.

2 Some children in Africa go swimming   **b** on cold and snowy days.

3 Some children go dog sledding   **c** on windy days.

27 **Put the words in order.**

1 active. | love | be | Kids | to

_____

2 windy, | a kite. | you | can | it's | When | fly

_____

3 rains. | when | Africa | In | children | it | swim

_____

4 make | snowy. | You | it's | can | snowmen | when

_____

5 snow. | the | in | pull | Dogs | sleds

_____

Do you like these sports? Write numbers to rate them.

THINK
BIG

1 = I love it!   2 = I like it.   3 = I don't like it.

_____ flying kites   _____ riding a bike

_____ playing volleyball   _____ swimming

_____ doing gymnastics   _____ playing soccer

_____ sledding   _____ running

_____ playing baseball

Read. Number the detail sentences 1 or 2 to go with topic sentence 1 or 2.

Topic sentence 1: *I like hot sunny weather.*

Topic sentence 2: *My best friend is Julie.*

☐ **a** I swim in the ocean on hot days.

☐ **b** Julie is in my class at school.

☐ **c** She wants to be a firefighter.

☐ **d** We play soccer together after school.

☐ **e** I like riding my bike in the sun.

☐ **f** I want to go to a desert.

 Write the best detail sentence to start each paragraph. Choose from the box.

Cats were everywhere!   I take care of my pet every day.   Math is fun.

1 Topic sentence: I have a pet.

Detail sentences: My pet's name is Tiny. He is a very small fish. He loves swimming every day.

_____

_____

2 Topic sentence: Math is my favorite subject.

Detail sentences: Math is easy for me. I help my friends with it.

_____

_____

30 **Read and circle sc, sw, sn, and sl.**

snail   snow   scout

coin   slow

sweet   foe

swim

scarf   sleep

31 **Underline the words with sc, sw, sn, and sl. Then read aloud.**

1 There is a swan sleeping on the swing.

2 Put on your scarf and put on your skiis. It's snowing!

32 **Connect the letters. Then write.**

1	sl	ail	**a**	_ _ _ _ _
2	sn	arf	**b**	_ _ _ _ _
3	sw	eep	**c**	_ _ _ _ _
4	sc	eet	**d**	_ _ _ _ _

33 **Listen and write.** 104

A ¹ _____

² _____ is eating

A ³ _____,

And a ⁴ _____

⁵ _____ is swimming.

34 **Read and choose.**

1 It's hot and dry there **because / so** it never rains.

2 **As / So** a result, few people live there.

3 The trees grow quickly because **of / to** the rainy climate.

4 **No / Not** many trees grow there because it's so hot.

5 Not many people live there **because of / few** the extreme temperature.

35 **Read and complete with is, isn't, was, wasn't.**

Emily: Hi, Sam. It ¹ _____ fun to see you yesterday.

Sam: Yes, I had fun, too.

Emily: What ² _____ the weather like this afternoon?

Sam: It was cool this morning, but it ³ _____ hot now.

Emily: It's the same here! It ⁴ _____ hot this morning,

but it is hot now.

Sam: That's funny. I am happy it ⁵ _____ rainy.

I don't like the rain.

Emily: I love the rain. I can watch TV!

Smells Good!

1 **Complete the sentences. Use words from the box.**

feels   looks   smell   sounds   tastes

1 My sweater _____ soft.

2 This pie _____ delicious.

3 This music _____ amazing.

4 My hair _____ terrible.

5 These flowers _____ nice.

2 **Write about you.**

1 What smells awful? _____

2 What smells wonderful? _____

3 Listen and number in order.

Grandma's House

We always do my favorite thing
Baking ginger cookies.
They taste so nice and yummy,
We are both very lucky! ☐

Yummy smells and her smiling face.
We really love my Grandma's place. ☐

We love my Grandma's house.
It always smells so nice.
It smells like ginger cookies
Sweet, with a little spice! ☐

Grandma likes playing old songs
From when she was very young.
The music sounds so wonderful,
We have to sing along. ☐

Chorus ☐

4 Look and read. Then circle.

1 How does the apple taste? It tastes **delicious** / **bad**.

2 How do these shoes feel? They feel **soft** / **tight**.

3 How does my hair look? It looks **terrible** / **nice**.

4 How does the band sound? The band sounds **bad** / **good**.

5 How do the flowers smell? They smell **awful** / **sweet**.

5 **Look and read. Then write Luke or Amy.**

It Tastes Terrible!

Luke smells the fish soup. He thinks it smells horrible. He thinks the soup looks bad, too. Amy tastes the soup and says, "It tastes... OK." Luke tries the soup. He says, "It tastes terrible." Amy has a cold. She can't smell or taste the soup.

1 _____ thinks the soup smells bad.
2 _____ thinks the soup doesn't look good.
3 _____ thinks the soup tastes OK.
4 _____ thinks the soup tastes terrible.
5 _____ can't taste or smell the soup.

6 **Think and write about you. Use smell or taste and the words from the box or your own ideas.**

I think _____ terrible.
I think _____ nice.
I think _____ horrible.
I think _____ delicious.

> a clean sock
> a flower   chocolate
> fish soup   ice cream

THINK BIG **Put in order.**

> awful   bad   good   great   OK

_____ very bad _____ _____ _____ very good _____

114

7 Listen and stick. Then number.

a

b

c

d

8 Read and circle. Then complete. Use the words from the box.

delicious   nice   quiet   soft   tight

1 I'm wearing my new shoes.

They **taste / feel** _____.

2 My baby brother isn't crying.

The house **tastes / sounds** _____.

3 I'm taking a walk in the garden.

The flowers **smell / sound** _____.

4 I'm eating my favorite lunch.

It **feels / tastes** _____.

5 You're wearing my new sweater.

It **looks / sounds** _____.

9 **Circle the correct word.**

1 How **do** / **does** the soup taste?

2 How **do** / **does** the pizza taste?

3 How **do** / **does** the sandals feel?

4 How **do** / **does** the apples smell?

5 How **do** / **does** the music sound?

6 How **do** / **does** the shirts look?

10 **Complete the questions. Then look and complete the answers.**

1 **A:** How _____ the sand feel?

B: It _____ hot.

2 **A:** How _____ the hat look?

B: It _____ pretty.

3 **A:** How _____ the birds sound?

B: They _____ loud.

4 **A:** How _____ the sandwiches taste?

B: They _____ delicious.

11 **Draw an interesting or funny cake. Color. Then write.**

1 How does it taste?

_____

2 How does it smell?

_____

3 How does it look?

_____

12 **Find and write the words.**

ensak

1 _____

haleoncem

2 _____

yutbferlt

3 _____

tab

4 _____

116
13 **Listen, read, and write.**

> brain   danger   echo   hear   senses   smell
> sound waves   taste buds   tastes   tongues

1   Our ¹ _____ are sending information to our ² _____ all the time. We need this information to know where we are and to understand the world around us.

2   Our senses keep us safe. For example, we can feel if something is hot or sharp. We can see and ³ _____ if we're in ⁴ _____. When we need food, our senses tell us if our food looks, smells, and ⁵ _____ good. Then we can decide if it's a good idea to eat it.

3   Animals have senses, too. They're very different from people's senses. We see with our eyes, but bats can't see well so they use their ears. They make sounds and listen for an ⁶ _____. The ⁷ _____ of the echo tell them where something is and its size.

4   Reptiles like snakes, lizards, and chameleons ⁸ _____ with their ⁹ _____ and not with their noses. They taste the air. Butterflies have tiny ¹⁰ _____ on their feet. They tell the butterfly what flower it's on. Then they know if they can eat it.

14 **Look at 13. Use the clues to complete the crossword puzzle.**

Across →

1 Snakes _____ with their tongues.

2 Butterflies _____ with their legs.

3 Our _____ keep us safe.

Down ↓

1 Bats use their ears to _____ things.

2 Chameleons use their _____ to catch food.

15 **Read and match.**

1 We understand the world around us

2 We can taste food and look at it

3 Animals use their senses, too,

4 A bat can see in the dark because

5 Reptiles taste the air around them

a it makes sounds and listens carefully.

b but they often use them differently.

c to know where there is food or danger.

d to know if it's good to eat.

e because our senses send information to our brain.

THINK BIG

Which animals use these senses? Match.

a
shark

b
elephant

c
tarsier

1 Because of its large ears, it has a very good sense of hearing. It also uses its trunk and feet to hear.

2 It uses its big eyes to find food at night.

3 It has a good sense of smell. It can smell food in the water from far away.

16 **Circle. Then write the answer.**

1

How **do / does** my hair look?

(It/great) _____.

2

How **do / does** the band sound?

(It/awful) _____.

3

How **do / does** the apple taste?

(It/great) _____.

4

How **do / does** your shoes feel?

(They/tight) _____.

5

How **do / does** your sweater feel?

(It/soft) _____.

6

How **do / does** the flowers smell?

(They/nice) _____.

17 **Read and write the answers.**

1 Does it sound OK? No, _____.

2 Do they look nice? No, _____.

3 Does it taste spicy? No, _____.

4 Does it sound like a violin? Yes, _____.

5 Does it feel soft? No, _____.

6 Do they taste salty? Yes, _____.

7 Does it smell like lemon? Yes, _____.

Grammar

18 **Write questions with How.**

1 your new iPod/sound

_____

2 my dress/look

_____

3 the jeans/feel

_____

4 the soup/taste

_____

5 her perfume/smell

_____

19 **Read and match.**

1	I have to wear a uniform.	**a**	It smells awful!
2	I got a jazz CD.	**b**	It tastes delicious.
3	Try the ice cream.	**c**	It feels tight.
4	I didn't take out the trash.	**d**	It looks good.
5	We painted his bedroom.	**e**	It sounds great!

20 **Put the words in order.**

1 | plays | every night. | in her room | She | her guitar |

_____

2 | a strange smell | in the garage | There | all the time. | is |

_____

3 | in the kitchen | tasted | before dinner. | the soup | He |

_____

4 | at 12:30 p.m. | at school | We always | a break for lunch | have |

_____

5 | in Spain | visit | every year. | They | their cousins |

_____

21 **Look, read, and match.**

a

b

c

d

1 trash collector

2 zoo keeper

3 baker

4 flower seller

119

22 **Read and write. Then listen and check.**

awful   bath   care   colors   fresh   sneeze   stinks   treats

1   André Tyrode is from Lyon. He makes cakes and pastries every day. He says everything he makes tastes and smells wonderful. He hates getting up early, but he loves the smell of [1] _____ bread. It makes him happy to make nice [2] _____ for people to eat.

2   Alberto Rivera is from Costa Rica and he grows and sells flowers on his farm. He sends them all over the world. He loves to smell the flowers and he likes their different [3] _____. Sometimes the flowers make him [4] _____. Flowers are beautiful, and they help him remember that the world is beautiful.

3   Candace Reilly is from Calgary in Canada. Her job is to pick up trash and help keep her city clean. It's a very important job, but the smell can be terrible. She says the trash really [5] _____ sometimes, but she's happy to make her city look better. She really likes her job.

4   Sarah Ang is from Singapore. She works at Singapore Zoo and takes [6] _____ of one of the largest Asian elephants in the world – Zelda. She often has to give her a [7] _____, and she gets wet, too. She says the smell can be [8] _____, but she likes taking care of her.

23 **Find and write the words.**

ekasc

losfewr

satipers

1 _____

2 _____

3 _____

walfu

nktiss

hatsr

4 _____

5 _____

6 _____

atbh

eesnez

ayerl

7 _____

8 _____

9 _____

24 **Look at 22. Match and write.**

1 André makes

2 Alberto grows

3 Candace picks up

4 Sarah washes

a flowers. They look _____.

b trash. It really _____.

c Zelda the elephant. Zelda smells _____.

d pastries. They taste _____.

THINK BIG

Do you like these jobs? Write numbers to rate them.

1 = I love it!   2 = I like it.   3 = I don't like it.

_____ Pick up trash.   _____ Grow and sell flowers.

_____ Make pastries.   _____ Work at a zoo.

25 **Read and circle T for true and F for false.**

1 A paragraph starts with a final sentence.   **T**   **F**

2 A topic sentence is the first sentence in a paragraph.   **T**   **F**

3 There are usually a few detail sentences in a paragraph.   **T**   **F**

4 A paragraph finishes with a title.   **T**   **F**

26 **Read. Match the final sentence to each paragraph.**

1 My favorite animals are sea lions. They sound funny. They can do great tricks and can swim.

2 Butterflies are interesting. They look beautiful, and they can fly. They taste with their legs!

3 My grandma's house smells good. Her cookies taste delicious. She plays the piano. The music sounds wonderful.

a They are my favorite insects!

b It's a great place to visit.

c They are wonderful animals.

27 **Write a final sentence.**

topic sentence → Lizards are amazing.

detail sentences →
Lizards can run fast.
Lizards smell with their tongues.
Lizards usually feel dry and cool.

final sentence → _____

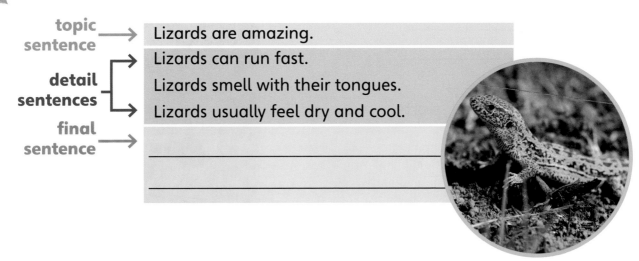

28 **Read and circle fl, pl, gl, and bl.**

> play   swan   slim
> flag   glad
> flip-flops   block
> glass   black
> plum

29 **Underline the words with fl, pl, gl, and bl. Then read aloud.**

1 There is a castle with a black flag.

2 Drink the glass of orange juice and eat the plum cake.

30 **Connect the letters. Then write.**

1 fl   um   **a** _ _ _ _
2 pl   ack   **b** _ _ _ _ _
3 gl   ag   **c** _ _ _ _
4 bl   ass   **d** _ _ _ _ _

124
31 **Listen and write.**

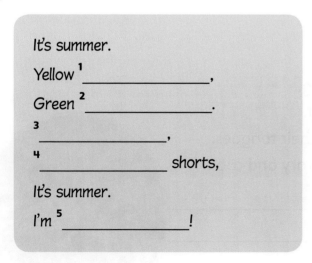

It's summer.
Yellow ¹_____,
Green ²_____.
³_____,
⁴_____ shorts,
It's summer.
I'm ⁵_____!

2 **Look and write.**

1 It _____ delicious.

2 They _____ good.

3 It _____ hot.

4 She _____ beautiful.

5 They _____ loud.

3 **Complete the questions and answer for you.**

1 _____ your hair look today?

_____

2 _____ new clothes feel?

_____

3 _____ a butterfly look?

_____

4 _____ your shoes feel?

_____

My hair looks bad today.

Max's Day at the Zoo

1 Look at the paths for Max's day at the zoo. Complete the sentences. Use words from the boxes.

ANIMALS
an owl
a shark
a camel

SENSES
sounds
looks
tastes
feels

START

Max

2 Look at the paths again. What do you think? Write the answers.

1 Animal Quiz

It doesn't live in oceans.

It lives in deserts.

It can't fly, but it can run fast.

What is it?

_____

2 What was the weather like?

Before the zoo, _____ .

After the zoo, _____ .

3 Choose one path. Draw the path. Learn about Max's day at the zoo.

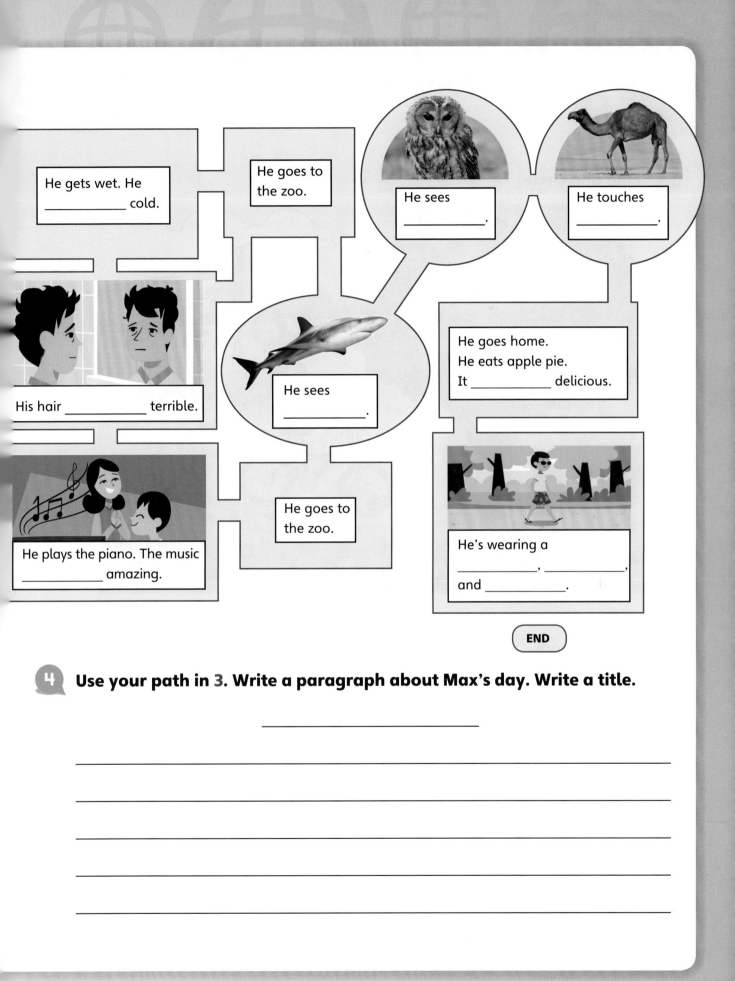

He gets wet. He _____ cold.

He goes to the zoo.

He sees _____.

He touches _____.

His hair _____ terrible.

He sees _____.

He goes home.
He eats apple pie.
It _____ delicious.

He plays the piano. The music _____ amazing.

He goes to the zoo.

He's wearing a _____, _____, and _____.

END

4 **Use your path in 3. Write a paragraph about Max's day. Write a title.**

_____

_____

_____

_____

_____

_____

unit 7 Fabulous Food!

1 Find and circle.

1 bread   **2** cheese   **3** green pepper   **4** lettuce

5 mushroom   **6** onions   **7** cucumbers   **8** pizza

9 tomatoes

2 Draw your favorite food and write.

Breakfast   Lunch   Dinner

For breakfast, I like eating _____

_____.

3 **Listen and circle the five incorrect words. Then listen and write.**

I'm Hungry!

Hi, Mom, I'm home from school.
I'm really hungry now.
I'd like to make a burger,
Can you show me how?

I am home from my school day.
I'd like a sandwich. Is that OK?

Are there any onions?
Here are some on the shelf.
Is there any mustard?
I see it for myself.

Chorus

There's just one problem, Mom
There isn't any lettuce!
But I have a great idea:
Let's have cake instead!

Chorus

1 _____

2 _____

3 _____

4 _____

5 _____

4 **Find and write. Then complete for you.**

1 **reneg speerpp** 2 **zizap**

_____ _____   _____

3 **rushmooms**   4 **atootm cause**

_____   _____ _____

I like _____ and _____.

I don't like _____ or _____.

5 **Read and write. Use the words from the box.**

A Surprise for Mom

Amy and Luke want to make dinner. It's a surprise for their mom. There's a green pepper, some cheese, and some olives. The cheese and olives are yummy, so Luke and Amy eat them. They take some more food out of the fridge. Mom comes home. The surprise isn't dinner. The surprise is a messy kitchen!

1 Amy and Luke are making _____ for their mom.

2 Amy and Luke eat the cheese and _____.

3 Amy and Luke find some more _____ in the fridge.

4 Their _____ isn't happy when she comes home.

5 Mom's surprise is a _____ kitchen.

> dinner
> food
> messy
> mom
> olives

6 **Look at the story picture in 5. Read and circle the correct answer.**

1 Is there a pineapple on the table?   **Yes, there is. / No, there isn't.**

2 Are there any mushrooms?   **Yes, there are. / No, there aren't.**

3 Is there any cheese?   **Yes, there is. / No, there isn't.**

4 Are there any olives on the table?   **Yes, there are. / No, there aren't.**

THINK BIG   **What do you need to make a cake? Find out and ✓.**

eggs ☐   butter ☐   cheese ☐   mushrooms ☐

sugar ☐   flour ☐   onions ☐   strawberries ☐

135

7 Listen and stick. Then listen and write the food.

1 _____

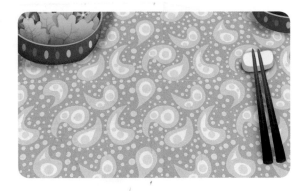

2 _____

3 _____

4 _____

8 Look and circle.

1 There **are some** / **aren't any** mushrooms.

2 There **is some** / **isn't any** mustard.

3 There **is some** / **isn't any** bread.

4 There **are some** / **aren't any** cucumbers.

5 There **is some** / **isn't any** lettuce.

6 There **are some** / **aren't any** green peppers.

9 **Look and answer. Use some or any.**

1 Is there any milk? _____

2 Is there any turkey? _____

3 Is there any tomato sauce? _____

4 Are there any eggs? _____

5 Are there any red peppers? _____

10 **Look at 9. Write the questions.**

1 _____   Yes, there is some cheese.

2 _____   Yes, there is some mustard.

3 _____   No, there aren't any onions.

4 _____   Yes, there are some green peppers.

5 _____   No, there isn't any juice.

11 **Read. Then write A, B, C, D, or E.**

	Where do we get the vitamins from?
Vitamin A	carrots, mangoes, milk, eggs
Vitamin B	potatoes, bread, chicken, cheese, eggs, green vegetables
Vitamin C	oranges, peppers, tomatoes, potatoes
Vitamin D	eggs, fish, milk, the sun
Vitamin E	nuts, green vegetables

1 Vitamin ____

2 Vitamin ____, ____, and ____

3 Vitamin ____

4 Vitamin ____

5 Vitamin ____ and ____

6 Vitamin ____

138
12 **Listen, read, and write.**

energy	good	healthy	important
naturally	strong	treats	

1   Vitamins are very **1** _____ for our bodies to stay **2** _____ and healthy. Vitamins are in food and drinks. You need to have vitamins every day. Vitamins A, D, and E live in the fat in our bodies. Vitamins C and B live in the water in our bodies.

2   Vitamin A is good for your eyes and skin. It's in orange and yellow fruits. Vitamin D makes our bones strong. Our body makes Vitamin D **3** _____ when it's in the sun. Vitamin E in nuts and green vegetables keeps your blood **4** _____. Vitamin C is **5** _____ for our bones, our teeth, and brain.

3   There are different kinds of Vitamin B, and they're in different foods. Some kinds give us **6** _____ for our muscles. Others help make blood. You can find vitamin B in some **7** _____, too, like dark chocolate!

13 **Look at 12. Read and circle.**

1 Vitamin A is good for our **eyes** / **ears**.

2 Vitamin B helps make blood and gives us **energy** / **skin**.

3 Vitamin C is good for bones, teeth, and our **brain** / **muscles**.

4 Vitamin D helps make strong **skin** / **bones**.

5 Vitamin E keeps our **blood** / **muscles** healthy.

14 **Read and match.**

1 Vitamins are in food and drinks and

2 Vitamins are very important if

3 The sun helps our body

4 There are different kinds of Vitamin B

5 Fruit and vegetables are good for you,

a make Vitamin D naturally.

b and you should try to have at least five a day.

c live in our body fat or water.

d we are to stay healthy.

e which give us energy or make our blood.

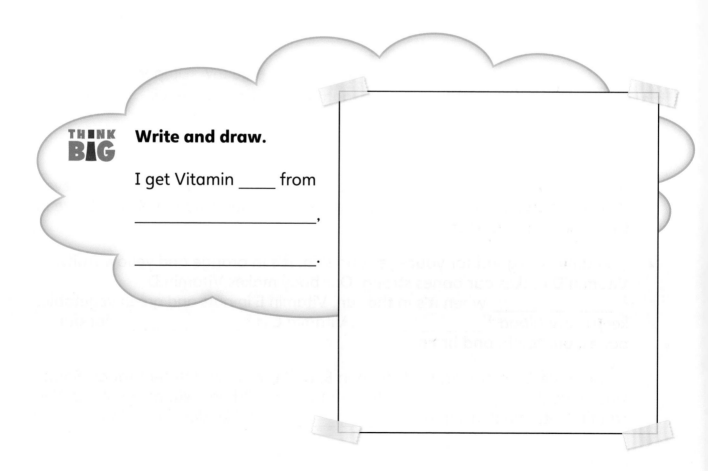

THINK BIG **Write and draw.**

I get Vitamin _____ from

_____,

_____.

15 **Write some, a, or an.**

1 I have _____ peppers.

2 I don't have _____ onion.

3 I have _____ milk.

4 I have _____ ketchup.

5 I don't have _____ egg.

6 I have _____ cheese.

7 I don't have _____ tomato.

8 I don't have _____ potato.

16 **Read the dialog and write. Use some, much, or many.**

I want to make
¹ _____ pancakes.

We don't have
² _____ eggs.

That's OK, we only need three. But we don't have
³ _____ milk.

I can get ⁴ _____ at the store.

Can you get ⁵ _____ maple syrup, too?

OK. But don't make too
⁶ _____ pancakes!

Grammar

17 **Read and circle.**

1 How **much** / **many** pizza do you want?

2 How **much** / **many** money do you have?

3 How **much** / **many** cookies are there?

4 How **much** / **many** ice cream would you like?

5 How **much** / **many** slices of pizza do you want?

6 How **much** / **many** fruit do you eat every day?

18 **Read and ✓.**

1 There's just ☐ a lot of   milk in the fridge, so don't use it all.
☐ a little
☐ a few

2 There aren't many cookies in the bag, there are just ☐ a lot of.
☐ a little.
☐ a few.

3 He bought ☐ a lot of   souvenirs, and now he has no money!
☐ a little
☐ a few

4 We only have ☐ a lot of   players for the game on Sunday.
☐ a little
☐ a few

5 I did ☐ a lot of   homework this evening, so now I want to take a rest.
☐ a little
☐ a few

19 **Look, read, and write the foods.**

> beans and toast   churros   huevos rancheros   rice, soup, and fish

Mexico   **Australia**   **Japan**   **Spain**

1 _____ 2 _____ 3 _____ 4 _____

141

20 **Listen, read, and write. Then check your answers in 19.**

> breakfast   cereal   delicious   donuts   meal
> pickles   sugar   toast   toasted

1   In the U.K., Katie's mom says ¹ _____ is the most important ² _____ of the day. On weekdays, Katie has cereal with milk and banana, boiled eggs with toast and marmite, or brown bread soldiers. On the weekend, she usually has bacon and tomato sandwiches. She doesn't like porridge, but her mom loves it.

2   Yoko is from Japan, and she never eats any ³ _____. In the morning, she usually eats rice, soup, fish, and ⁴ _____.

3   Luis, from Spain, likes to eat bread or cereal when he gets up. Sometimes on the weekend, he has churros with chocolate. Churros are like little ⁵ _____.

4   In Mexico, Camilla often eats fried eggs for breakfast. In Spanish, they're called huevos rancheros, and she puts them on ⁶ _____ tortillas with some salsa. They're spicy, colorful, and taste ⁷ _____.

5   Tony in Australia also likes marmite (it's brown and salty, and you can put it on your ⁸ _____). He also eats porridge, and puts cream and some brown ⁹ _____ on top. He loves eating beans on toast in the morning.

21 **Look at 20. Circle T for true and F for false.**

1   Katie has bacon and marmite sandwiches.   T   F

2   Yoko never eats rice or fish for breakfast.   T   F

3   Luis sometimes eats churros with chocolate.   T   F

4   Camila eats salsa with her huevos rancheros.   T   F

5   Tony has brown sugar on his toast.   T   F

22 **Put the words in order.**

1   is   breakfast   very   good   A   important.

_____

2   porridge.   honey   mom   on   Katie's   likes   her

_____

3   usually   rice,   fish.   has   soup,   Yoko   and

_____

4   has   churros,   Luis   sometimes   eats   eggs.   but   usually

_____

5   to   toast   beans   likes   on   eat   top.   Tony   with

_____

Draw a picture of your favorite breakfast and write.

THINK BIG

My favorite breakfast is

_____.

It's important to eat a
good breakfast because

_____

_____.

title ⟶ **My Favorite Breakfast**
by Laura Brown

topic sentence ⟶ I like a lot of different things for breakfast, but I have my favorite breakfast every Sunday morning.

detail sentences ⟶ I start with some orange slices, cold from the fridge. Then my mother makes two fluffy pancakes for me. I put butter on them, and then I put warm maple syrup on top. The pancakes are delicious with a glass of cold milk.

final sentence ⟶ My favorite breakfast makes Sundays special.

23 **Write. Use the words from the box.**

detail sentences   final sentence   title   topic sentence

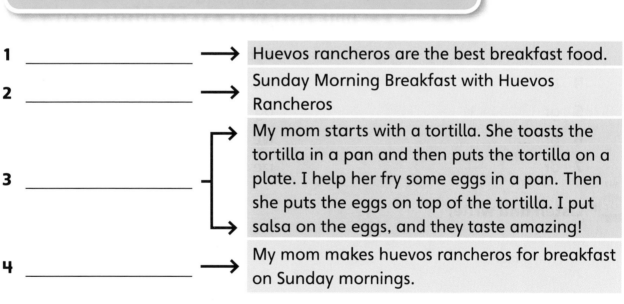

1 _____ ⟶ Huevos rancheros are the best breakfast food.

2 _____ ⟶ Sunday Morning Breakfast with Huevos Rancheros

3 _____ ⟶ My mom starts with a tortilla. She toasts the tortilla in a pan and then puts the tortilla on a plate. I help her fry some eggs in a pan. Then she puts the eggs on top of the tortilla. I put salsa on the eggs, and they taste amazing!

4 _____ ⟶ My mom makes huevos rancheros for breakfast on Sunday mornings.

24 **Look at 23. Write the paragraph in order.**

_____

_____

_____

_____

_____

25 **Read and circle br, cr, dr, fr, gr, pr, and tr.**

bread   grass   **dream**   glad

frog

cream   plant   prize   train

26 **Underline the words with br, cr, dr, fr, gr, pr, and tr. Then read aloud.**

1 The frog's driving the green and brown train.

2 She's crying because she got a prize and she's happy.

27 **Connect the letters. Then write.**

1	br	eam	**a** _ _ _ _ _
2	cr	oll	**b** _ _ _ _ _
3	fr	ead	**c** _ _ _ _ _
4	tr	ass	**d** _ _ _ _ _
5	gr	og	**e** _ _ _ _
6	pr	ive	**f** _ _ _ _ _
7	dr	ize	**g** _ _ _ _ _

147

28 **Listen and write.**

Every night,
I ¹_____
About a ²_____
And a ³_____,
And a ⁴_____
⁵_____!
In my dream,
They eat ⁶_____
With ⁷_____.

9 Look. Then circle the different kinds of food.

1

The sandwich has:

bread   green peppers
tomatoes   mustard
turkey   onions
cheese   lettuce

2

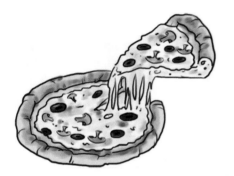

The pizza has:

mustard   lettuce
cheese   olives
tomato sauce   ice cream
chicken   mushrooms

3

The salad has:

tomato sauce   cucumbers
turkey   milk
lettuce   cheese
onions   chicken
green peppers   tomatoes

10 Look at 29 and answer.

1 Is there any lettuce in the sandwich? _____

2 Is there any mustard on the pizza? _____

3 Are there any olives on the pizza? _____

4 Are there any onions in the salad? _____

11 Write about your home.

1 Are there any tomatoes in your fridge? _____

2 Is there any milk in your fridge? _____

unit 8 Healthy Living

1 Write. Use activities from the box. Then ✓ the healthy ones.

| ate a healthy breakfast | ate pie for breakfast | drank lots of water |
| got ten hours of sleep | got two hours of sleep | rode a bike |

1 _____
_____ ☐

2 _____
_____ ☐

3 _____
_____ ☐

4 _____
_____ ☐

5 _____
_____ ☐

6 _____
_____ ☐

2 Read and circle for you.

1 How do you feel today? I feel **great** / **awful** / **OK** today.

2 Did you get enough sleep? **Yes** / **No**

3 Did you eat any breakfast? **Yes** / **No**

4 Did you drink lots of water? **Yes** / **No**

5 Did you ride your bike? **Yes** / **No**

6 Did you have a healthy lunch? **Yes** / **No**

7 Did you do any exercise? **Yes** / **No**

3 Listen and write.

| any | Did | enough | good | too | you |

Live Right!

Did you eat breakfast? asks Mom,
You don't look ¹_____ to me.
Did you get ²_____ sleep? asks Mom,
Did you watch ³_____much TV?

**Enough sleep. Good food.
Be healthy. Live right!
Enough sleep. Good food.
Be healthy. Live right!**

⁴_____ you ride your bike? asks Mom,
You know it's good for ⁵_____.
Did you get ⁶_____ exercise?
You know it's good to do!

Chorus

4 Read and ✓ for you. Then answer with Yes, I did or No, I didn't.

My Habits Last Week	Sun	Mon	Tue	Wed	Thu	Fri	Sat
1 got enough sleep							
2 drank enough water							
3 ate healthy food							

Did you get enough sleep? _____

Did you drink enough water? _____

Did you eat enough healthy food? _____

5 **Read and answer. Write Yes, she did or No, she didn't.**

An Unhealthy Dinner

Amy's dad wants her to be healthy. Amy likes unhealthy food. She ate a burger and fries for her dinner. Fried food isn't healthy. She drank a large cola. Cola isn't healthy. It has a lot of sugar. Now, Amy doesn't feel very well.

1 Did Amy eat a burger and fries for dinner? _____

2 Did she eat fried food? _____

3 Did she drink a large glass of water? _____

4 Did she eat a healthy dinner? _____

6 **What did you eat for dinner yesterday? Was it healthy? Draw, write, and circle.**

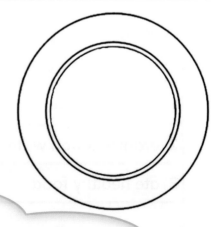

Yesterday for dinner, I ate _____

and I drank _____.

My dinner **was / wasn't** healthy.

Healthy or unhealthy? Draw.

THINK BIG

fries   lettuce   tomatoes   bottle of cola   burger   water

156
7 **Listen and stick. What did Grace and Carlos do on the weekend?**

Sunday

1 _____

Saturday

Sunday

2 _____   3 _____

8 **Read and complete with did or didn't.**

1 **Lou:** Are you feeling OK?

Jack: I'm tired.

Lou: _____ you exercise today?

Jack: No, I _____. I played video games all day.

Lou: Oh. _____ you sleep eight hours?

Jack: No, I _____. I slept four hours.

2 **Ellen:** Hi, Jim. I feel great today! How are you?

Jim: Not good. I _____ eat a good breakfast.

Ellen: What _____ you eat?

Jim: I ate ice cream, and I drank cola.

Ellen: Really? What _____ you eat for lunch?

Jim: I forgot lunch. I _____ eat lunch.

Language in Action

9 **Look and circle.**

| Yesterday Morning | Yesterday Afternoon | Yesterday Evening |

1 They **ate dinner** / **woke up** yesterday evening.

2 They **watched TV** / **woke up** yesterday afternoon.

3 They **ate dinner** / **woke up** yesterday morning.

10 **Look and answer.**

1 Did he get enough sleep? _____

2 Did she get enough sleep? _____

3 Did they get enough exercise? _____

4 Did she eat a healthy dinner? _____

5 Did he eat a healthy dinner? _____

6 Did she drink any water? _____

7 Did he drink enough water? _____

11 **Read and complete. Use the words from the box.**

> active   activities   energy   measure   put on weight   watching TV

A calorie is a ¹_____ of the energy we get from food. We need calories to give us ²_____ to do different activities and sports. Some ³_____ , such as riding a bike and dancing, use a lot of calories and are really good for us. Sleeping and ⁴_____ don't use any calories. If we eat more calories than we use, we can ⁵_____ , so it's important to stay ⁶_____ .

158
12 **Read and circle. Then listen and check.**

1   It's important to eat, exercise, rest, and sleep every day. Food and drinks give us energy because they have **¹ muscles / calories** in them. A calorie is a **² measure / activity** of this energy.

2   Some foods have a lot of calories and some don't. We need to have a certain number of calories to be **³ fat / healthy**. If we have too many calories and don't use the energy, we can **⁴ take / put on** weight and become **⁵ tired / fat**. Exercise uses the energy by burning calories.

3   Being active and doing exercise at any age is also good for the heart, our **⁶ bones / feet**, and our **⁷ teeth / muscles**. Activities like swimming, bike riding, dancing, running, and walking are good for burning calories and keeping us in shape. Sitting down at the computer too much or watching too much TV isn't good for your body.

4   Sleeping is important to give your body and brain time to **⁸ play / rest**. The next day we can continue to be active and work or study. Too much or too little sleep can be bad for your **⁹ exercise / health**. Doctors say between 9 and 10 hours of sleep is best for teenagers.

5   We always have to try to find time to **¹⁰ watch television / exercise** and to rest. We always have to watch what we eat. It's OK to have candy or chocolate from time to time, but, since they have a lot of calories, they aren't healthy foods.

13 **Look at 12. Read and match.**

1 Calories are measures of energy

2 When we are active, our body

3 Bike riding or walking is good for us,

4 Too many calories

5 Sleep is important because

a can make us fat if we don't exercise.

b but watching too much TV is unhealthy.

c our body and brain can rest.

d and are in the things we eat and drink.

e burns calories to take the energy we need.

14 **Complete the diagram. Add five more activities.**

dancing   doing gymnastics   playing basketball   playing video games
playing tennis   riding a bike   running   sleeping   watching a DVD

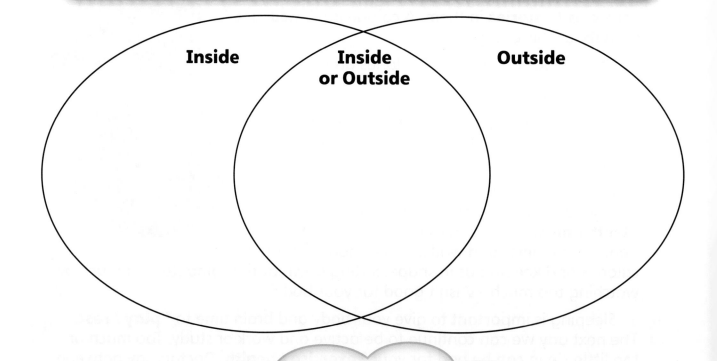

Inside

Inside or Outside

Outside

 THINK BIG   **Read and choose.**

1 Sleep for **eight / twelve** hours a day.

2 Play **six hours / one hour** of soccer a day.

3 Eat a **big / small** breakfast.

15 **Complete the chart. Use the words from the box.**

> arrive   clap   control   cook   dry   fry   jog
> live   look   love   study   work

climb**ed**	tr**ied**	change**d**	drop**ped**

16 **Read and write.**

1 eat _____*ate*_____

2 get _____

3 hurt _____

4 make _____

5 ride _____

6 run _____

7 say _____

8 sit _____

9 swim _____

10 wake _____

17 **Read and write. Use the correct form of the verb in parentheses.**

When Josh ¹ _____ (come) home, he ² _____ (go) to bed
and ³ _____ (sleep) for ten hours. He ⁴ _____ (be) so tired.
When he ⁵ _____ (get) up, he ⁶ _____ (eat) a big breakfast
and then ⁷ _____ (ride) his bike for an hour. He ⁸ _____
(visit) his favorite café and ⁹ _____ (drink) some apple juice. He
¹⁰ _____ (see) some friends in the afternoon. In the evening, he
¹¹ _____ (clean) his room and then ¹² _____ (start) to watch
a movie. But he ¹³ _____ (fall) asleep in the first ten minutes!

18 **Complete the questions and answers.**

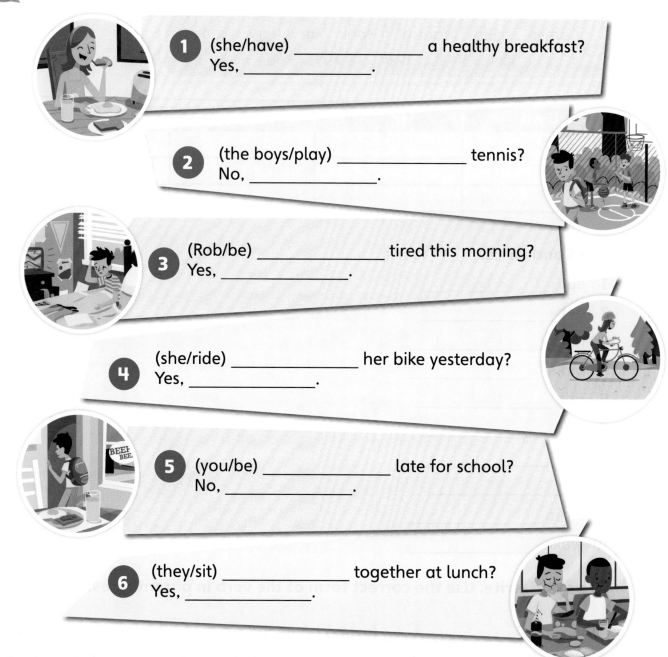

1 (she/have) _____ a healthy breakfast?
Yes, _____.

2 (the boys/play) _____ tennis?
No, _____.

3 (Rob/be) _____ tired this morning?
Yes, _____.

4 (she/ride) _____ her bike yesterday?
Yes, _____.

5 (you/be) _____ late for school?
No, _____.

6 (they/sit) _____ together at lunch?
Yes, _____.

19 **Write negative sentences.**

1 He drank lots of water.

_____

2 We forgot to invite the neighbors.

_____

3 They got a letter from the bank.

_____

20 **Look at 21. Read quickly and match.**

Octopush

Pumpkin Regatta

Footvolley

1 Octopush is like hockey,

2 A pumpkin regatta is like a boat race,

3 Footvolley is like volleyball,

a but people don't race in boats.

b but the players use a soccer ball.

c but people play it under water.

161

21 **Listen, read, and write.**

> kick   net   regattas   rowing   score   Teams

1   Octopush is like hockey, but people play it underwater in a swimming pool. A scuba diving club invented it in 1954 when it was too cold to go in the ocean. The game started in England, but now people play it all over the world. You need eight players to play. ¹ _____ use sticks to push a puck or "squid" into a net to ² _____ points.

2   Footvolley is just like volleyball, but players use a soccer ball. The game started in Brazil on Copacabana Beach in 1965. Police always stopped people playing soccer on the beach, so people played on volleyball courts instead. They invented footvolley. You have to ³ _____ the ball over the ⁴ _____, and you can't touch it with your hands. It's exciting but difficult. Many famous Brazilian soccer players also play footvolley.

3   In the fall, in parts of the United States and Canada, there's a contest called a Pumpkin Regatta. It's a boat race, but people use giant, hollowed out pumpkins instead! It started in 1999 in Windsor in Nova Scotia. A man there grew giant pumpkins, and he decided to use them for ⁵ _____. Pumpkin racing became very popular, and soon other places raced their own ⁶ _____. The pumpkins weigh more than 450 kilograms. After the race, there's usually a pumpkin pie-eating contest.

22 **Read and match.**

1 Scuba divers in England started octopush

2 In octopush, the players use sticks

3 Footvolley started when the police stopped

4 A man grew giant pumpkins

5 When the races finish,

a people playing soccer on the beach.

b and hollowed them out to use them as boats.

c because the ocean was too cold.

d people eat pumpkin pies.

e to push a puck into the net to score.

23 **Read and circle T for true and F for false.**

1 Octopush is a game where you need eight points to win. T F

2 In footvolley, you can use your hands and your feet. T F

3 The police said the people couldn't play soccer on the beach. T F

4 In a pumpkin regatta, people row their boats to race against pumpkins. T F

5 After regattas, people eat pumpkin pie. T F

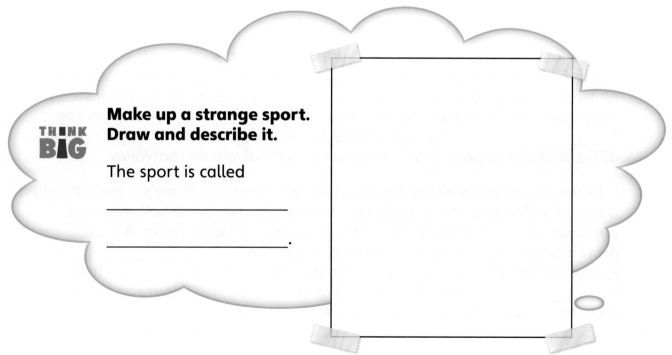

THINK BIG

Make up a strange sport. Draw and describe it.

The sport is called

_____

_____ .

24 **Read and circle.**

1 I usually walk to school, **or** / **but** today I rode my bike.

2 I sometimes play tennis **and** / **but** baseball after school.

3 I can walk to school, **or** / **but** I can take a bus to school.

4 I like dancing, **and** / **but** I'm not very good at it.

5 I usually get eight **and** / **or** nine hours of sleep.

6 It's hot **but** / **and** sunny today.

25 **Read and write. Use the ideas from the box.**

> and I help her do the dishes
> but he isn't good at basketball
> but she sounds terrible
> or I take the bus

1 My friend always plays the guitar, _____.

2 My brother is good at flying kites, _____.

3 My dad drives me to school, _____.

4 I help my mom cook dinner, _____.

26 **Read and complete with or, but, or and.**

I think I live a healthy life. I love doing exercise [1]_____ playing sports. I usually play tennis [2]_____ volleyball on Saturday, [3]_____ when it's rainy I go running inside in a gym. I sometimes have a burger [4]_____ fries for lunch, [5]_____ I usually eat turkey and rice [6]_____ pizza and salad.

27 **Read and circle all, au, and aw.**

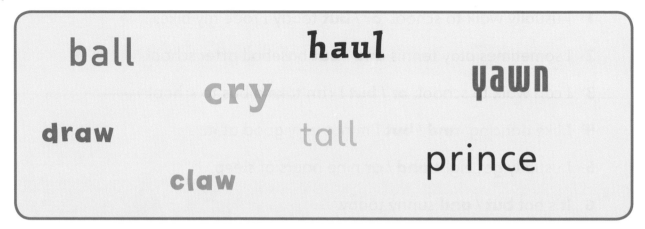

ball

haul

cry

yawn

draw

tall

prince

claw

28 **Underline the words with all, au, and aw. Then read aloud.**

1 Paul, don't kick the ball to the wall.

2 Draw a tiger with big claws.

29 **Connect the letters. Then write.**

1 sm   aul   **a** _ _ _ _

2 dr   all   **b** _ _ _ _ _

3 h   aw   **c** _ _ _ _

30 **Listen and write.**
167

I'm ¹ _____, I'm bored.
Yawn, ² _____.
Let's play, let's play
With a ³ _____,
Let's ⁴ _____,
Let's draw a ⁵ _____.

31 **Circle the correct verb.**

1 Did they **eat** / **ate** a healthy lunch?

2 She **drink** / **drank** enough water today.

3 She didn't **play** / **played** volleyball today.

32 **Read and complete. Use the words from the box.**

> any   didn't   enough   got   healthy   rode

1 John didn't get _____ sleep last night. He woke up at 4 a.m.

2 John _____ eat breakfast this morning.

3 John didn't get _____ exercise today. He watched TV all day.

4 Sue _____ enough sleep last night.

5 Sue ate a _____ breakfast this morning.

6 Sue _____ her bike to school today.

33 **Complete the sentences. Use the words in parentheses.**

1 _____ soccer is a lot of fun and it's good for my health. (play)

2 _____ is good for your body. (run)

3 _____ my bike is good for my health. (ride)

4 _____ is important. But don't sleep too much! (sleep)

5 _____ turkey and rice is good for me. (eat)

unit 9 School Trips!

1 **Look and write.**

> aquarium   art gallery   dairy farm   museum   national park   zoo

1 _____

2 _____

3 _____

4 _____

5 _____

6 _____

2 **Look, read, and circle. Then number.**

1 We went to a national park. We learned about
   a penguins.   **b** rocks.   **c** music.

2 We went to the zoo. We saw
   a dinosaurs.   **b** elephants.   **c** paintings.

3 We went to a dairy farm. We learned about
   a rocks.   **b** paintings.   **c** cows.

4 We went to a concert hall. We heard
   a some music.   **b** sea lions.   **c** some cows.

3 Listen and number in order.

Learning Out of School

Where did you go?
What did you see?
We went to the zoo, we saw a play,
We had a great time!

I like going on school trips,
Learning out of school.
We go to lots of places.
They're interesting and cool!

**School trips. School trips.
They're a lot of fun.
School trips. School trips.
Let's go on one!**

Aquarium, theater, concert hall, and zoo,
We saw some great things.
There was lots to do!

Chorus

4 Write.

My favorite school trip is _____.

5 Read and write.

> art gallery   concert hall   dairy farm   theater   zoo

1   I didn't see any giraffes, but I saw a hippo and zebra.
    _____

2   I learned about French artists. _____

3   I saw a play about animals. _____

4   We saw about five hundred cows! They were
    smelly. _____

5   There were drums, violins, and guitars there and the
    music was great. _____

6 **Read. Then write Luke or Amy.**

A Cool Trip

Luke and Amy went on a trip. They went to the Red Rock National Park. They learned about many kinds of rocks. Amy liked the trip a lot. Luke didn't like the trip. He didn't like the rocks, and he didn't like walking. Amy got a present for Luke. It was a rock!

1 _____ really liked the trip.

2 _____ didn't like the trip.

3 _____ didn't like the rocks.

4 _____ got a present for her brother.

7 **Imagine a school trip. Then answer.**

1 Where did you go?

_____

2 When did you go?

_____

3 What did you see?

_____

4 Did you like the trip?

_____

What happens next in the story? Write.

THINK
BIG

_____

_____

_____

176

8 Listen and stick.

a

b

c

d
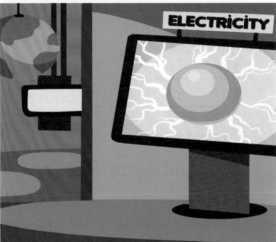

9 **Write. Complete the dialog.**

A: Where ¹_____ you go on
your school trip?

B: We ²_____ to a dairy farm.

A: What ³_____ you see?

B: We saw farmers milk cows.

A: Did you ⁴_____ it?

B: No, I ⁵_____.
The cows smelled awful!

10 **Think about a trip you took. Draw and answer.**

Where did you go?

You: _____

What did you see?

You: _____

What did you do?

You: _____

11 **Complete. Then match.**

> heard   learned   saw (x2)

1 _____ a movie about dinosaurs   **a** national park

2 _____ a play about animals   **b** concert hall

3 _____ about rocks and nature   **c** museum

4 _____ some music   **d** theater

12 **Read and match. Make questions.**

1 What   **a** did they go?

2 Did   **b** did they see?

3 Where   **c** they like it?

13 **Look at 12. Write the questions. Imagine the answers.**

1 **A:** _____

   B: _____

2 **A:** _____

   B: _____

3 **A:** _____

   B: _____

14 **Look at the paintings. Match.**

a    b    c    d

1 *Old Man with his Head in his Hands*, by Vincent Van Gogh.

2 *Haystacks at Giverny*, by Claude Monet.

3 *Spring 1573*, by Giuseppe Arcimboldo.

4 *The Little Giants*, by Francisco de Goya.

178
15 **Listen, read, and write.**

> century   copy   Dutch   impressionist
> Museum   nature   painting   watercolor

1   On her visit to the National Gallery, Amy's favorite ¹ _____ was *Spring 1573* by Giuseppe Arcimboldo. Arcimboldo was an Italian artist and he painted *Spring 1573* in the 16th century. He painted a face that has fruit, vegetables, and flowers. It's very smart because it shows the connection between people and ² _____. Amy thought it was pretty and colorful.

2   Nina loves a painting called *The Little Giants* from the Prada ³ _____ in Madrid. It's by the Spanish artist Francisco de Goya. It's from the 19th ⁴ _____ and shows some children playing a game. The young children are happy, but the older children look sad. The artist lost his hearing soon after he finished this painting.

3   Asya likes the painting *Haystacks at Giverny* by Claude Monet. He was a French ⁵ _____ painter. The original is in the Musée d'Orsay in Paris. Asya's grandmother has a ⁶ _____ of it in her living room. The picture shows a farm, she thinks, and makes her think of summer.

4   Idris likes *Old Man with his Head in his Hands* by Vincent Van Gogh. Van Gogh was ⁷ _____ and the painting is in a museum near where he lived. It's a sketch with ⁸ _____ from 1882. He finds it sad to look at but also interesting. He thinks something bad happened, so it scares him a little. Van Gogh was very sick when he painted it.

16 **Look at 15. Circle T for true and F for false.**

1 *Spring 1573* is a picture of a person's face with food and flowers.　　**T**　　**F**

2 All the children in *The Little Giants* are happy.　　**T**　　**F**

3 The artist Francisco de Goya went deaf.　　**T**　　**F**

4 Asya's grandmother has a copy of *Haystacks at Giverny* in her house.　　**T**　　**F**

5 *Old Man with his Head in his Hands* is an oil painting.　　**T**　　**F**

6 Idris doesn't feel happy when he looks at the painting by Van Gogh.　　**T**　　**F**

17 **Read and match.**

1 Amy thinks the painting is smart because

2 In the painting, there are some children playing,

3 The painting makes Asya think

4 Van Gogh's painting is a sketch in watercolor,

a it shows a connection between people and nature.

b of summer.

c so it wasn't made with oils.

d but some look happy and some look sad.

Choose one of the painters. Find out information about one more of his paintings and write.

THINK BIG

The painting's name is _____, and it was painted in _____ by _____. In the painting, there is/are _____ and _____. I think the painting looks _____.

18 **Read and write. Use the past tense of the verbs in parentheses.**

The school trip ¹ _____ (be) great.
We ² _____ (visit) the zoo. We
³ _____ (see) lots of animals and
⁴ _____ (learn) a lot. Some monkeys
⁵ _____ (jump) on our bus! They
⁶ _____ (like) playing with us. We
⁷ _____ (try) to get them off, but
they ⁸ _____ (stay) on the bus all
the time! Then, we ⁹ _____ (stop)
at the café to rest. We ¹⁰ _____
(drink) some water and ¹¹ _____
(have) a little snack to eat. We
¹² _____ (be) so hungry! After
our break, we ¹³ _____ (go) around the reptile house.
I liked the big snakes. I ¹⁴ _____ (get) a DVD from the souvenir shop.

19 **Look at 18. Make negative sentences.**

1 The school trip _____ great.

2 We _____ the zoo.

3 Some monkeys _____ on our bus.

4 They _____ playing with us.

5 We _____ to get them off.

6 They _____ on the bus all the time.

7 We _____ at the café.

8 We _____ water and we _____ a snack.

9 I _____ the big snakes.

10 I _____ a DVD from the souvenir shop.

Grammar

20 **Make questions and write answers.**

1 you visit/aquarium/on Saturday

    A: _Did you visit the aquarium on Saturday?_ _____?

          ✗ aquarium   ✓ zoo

    B: _I didn't visit the aquarium, but I visited the zoo._ _____.

2 he go/theater/last night

    A: _____?

          ✗ theater   ✓ movies

    B: _____.

3 they play/computer games/last weekend

    A: _____?

          ✗ computer games   ✓ chess

    B: _____.

4 she see/*The Lego Movie*/yesterday

    A: _____?

          ✗ *The Lego Movie*   ✓ *The Boxtrolls*

    B: _____.

5 you buy/T-shirt/this morning

    A: _____?

          ✗ T-shirt   ✓ sweater

    B: _____.

21 **Write questions using Why.**

1 Her teacher wasn't at school today.

    Why wasn't her teacher at school today? _____

2 You didn't get the bus.

    _____

3 She didn't call the police.

    _____

4 He didn't get more eggs.

    _____

22 **Look and write.**

> flamenco   Mua Roi Nuoc   Shakespeare play

1 _____   2 _____   3 _____

181

23 **Read and write. Then listen and check.**

> actors   audiences   magical   Movies   plays   shows   stage   theater

1   People love entertainment. **¹** _____ and TV are new kinds of entertainment, but entertainment on **²** _____ is much older. Theaters are still very popular all over the world.

2   The Greeks had theaters more than 2,000 years ago, almost in every city. The **³** _____ had important things to say about life. They were sometimes funny or sad, and only had men or boys as **⁴** _____. They usually had a chorus with people singing. Greek plays are still popular today.

3   Going to the **⁵** _____ became very popular about 400 years ago because of William Shakespeare. He wrote many different and smart plays, which people still watch and love today. People laugh or feel sad about the same things as the **⁶** _____ of his time. One of his most famous plays is *Romeo and Juliet*.

4   Stage **⁷** _____ with music and dance are also very popular. In Spain, people enjoy flamenco music and dance. There's usually a guitar player and one or more singers. Then there are the palmeros, who sing and clap in a special way, while men and women dance. There's a story, and the dancing and music are very dramatic.

5   Mua Roi Nuoc is theater entertainment in Vietnam. The performances use only puppets on a stage filled with water. These shows began in the 11th century and people still watch them today. They're **⁸** _____.

24 **Read and match.**

1 Movies and TV
   are popular,

2 Greek plays were
   funny or sad

3 William Shakespeare
   wrote many plays

4 Flamenco dancing
   in Spain

5 Mua Roi Nuoc
   in Vietnam

a usually goes with guitar
   music and clapping.

b but they aren't as old
   as theater entertainment.

c is very old and only
   uses puppets.

d and made going to
   the theater popular.

e and usually had a
   chorus with singing.

25 **Find the words. Use them to complete the sentences.**

> atesg   earteth   ncdae   upeptsp   ylsap

1 Flamenco is a Spanish _____.

2 Mua Roi Nuoc is a Vietnamese show with _____.

3 _____ became popular in England 400 years ago.

4 William Shakespeare's _____ are still very popular today.

5 The music for flamenco is usually played on a _____.

What stories do you like in movies or theater? Happy, sad, romantic, action, or adventure? Write three sentences about why you like them.

THINK
BIG
_____

_____

_____

26 **Underline subjects in red, verbs in blue, and objects in purple.**

1 Sally and Craig went to the zoo.

2 I didn't see a sea lion show.

3 My parents went out for dinner.

4 We visited an art gallery.

5 Did you see any rocks?

27 **What's missing? Write S for subject, V for verb, and O for object. Then look and complete.**

| I learned like paintings they |

1 They saw lots of _____. ☐

2 We didn't _____ the play. ☐

3 _____ watched a movie today. ☐

4 Ali and Peter _____ about dinosaurs. ☐

5 Did _____ like it? ☐

28 **Put the paragraph in order. Now write your own.**

At my school, we go on school trips every month.

I want to go again. It was a lot of fun!

A Trip to the Aquarium ☐

First, we saw penguins and turtles. Then we saw lots of sharks. These were my favorite. There was a whale show and it was amazing. I took some pictures and we loved it.

_____

_____

_____

_____

29 **Read and circle nt, ld, nd, and st.**

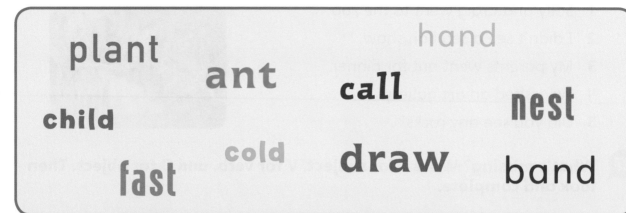

plant

ant

hand

call

child

nest

cold

draw

fast

band

30 **Underline the words with nt, ld, nd, and st. Then read aloud.**

1 Put your hands in your pockets. It's cold.

2 This is an ant's nest.

31 **Connect the letters. Then write.**

1 pla   ld   **a** _ _ _ _

2 co   nd   **b** _ _ _ _

3 ha   st   **c** _ _ _ _

4 ne   nt   **d** _ _ _ _ _

187

32 **Listen and write.**

An **1** _____,

2 _____

3 _____ playing

In the **4** _____.

A **5** _____

6 _____ playing in

A **7** _____.

33 **Read the clues and write the places.**

1 The paintings were beautiful here.

_____

2 I learned about penguins and zebras.

_____

3 The music sounds amazing.

_____

4 We saw sea lions and sharks.

_____

34 **Find the five adjectives. Use them to make sentences.**

avuwfunnysfionboringjomsinterestingxicqscaryeapostrangetyur

1 I think _____ **is / are** _____ because _____

_____.

2 I think _____.

3 I _____.

4 _____

5 _____

35 **Complete the dialogs.**

1 **A:** My parents ¹_____ to a play last night. (go)

B: ²_____ they like it? (do)

A: Yes, they ³_____! (do)

B: ⁴_____ you in the play? (be)

A: Yes, I ⁵_____! (be)

2 **A:** Where ¹_____ you yesterday? (be)

B: We ²_____ to the museum. (go)

A: Did you ³_____ fun? (have)

B: No, we ⁴_____. (do not) We ⁵_____ it. (not like)

Matt's Day

1 **Look at the paths for Matt's day and complete the faces.**

= healthy   = unhealthy

2 **Choose one path. Draw the path. Learn about Matt's day.**

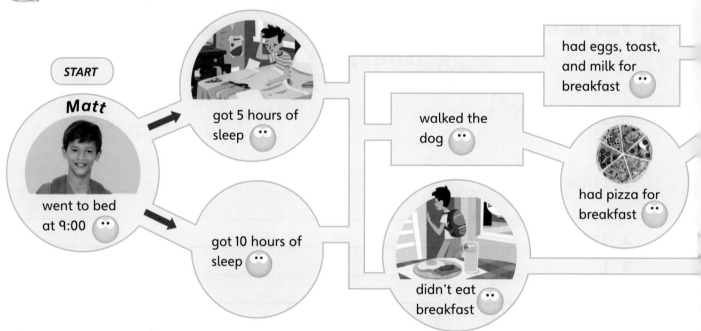

3 **Look at your path in 2. What do you think? Write the answers.**

1 What time did Matt wake up? _____

2 Did Matt get enough sleep? _____

3 Did Matt get enough exercise? _____

4 Did Matt eat healthy food? _____

5 Where did Matt go on the school trip? What did he do? _____

_____

6 How did Matt feel in the evening? _____

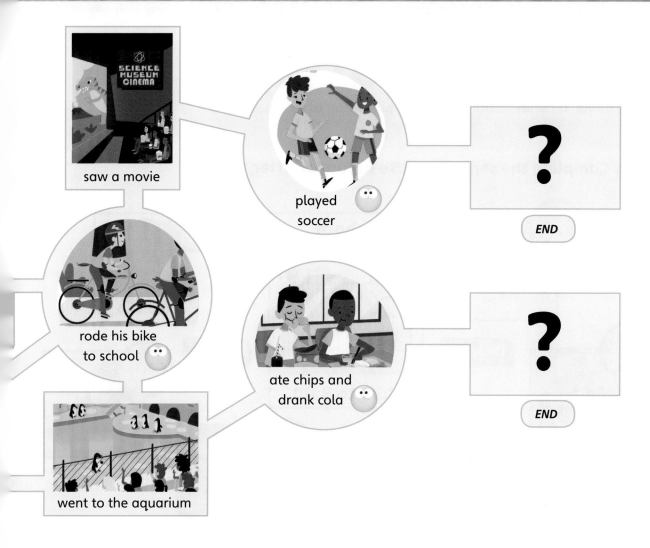

4 **Use your path in 2. Write a paragraph about Matt's day. Write a title.**

_____

_____

_____

_____

_____

_____

_____

_____

What does he/she do **before** school?	He/She eats breakfast **before** school.
What do you do **after** school?	I play soccer **after** school.

1 **Look. Complete the sentences. Use before or after.**

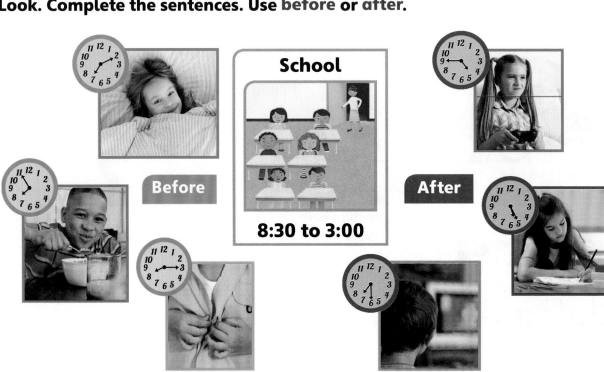

School

Before

8:30 to 3:00

After

1 She plays video games _____ school.

2 What does she do _____ school? She wakes up.

3 She always gets dressed _____ school.

4 What does he have _____ school? He has cereal.

5 He always watches TV _____ school.

6 What does she do _____ school? She does her homework.

2 **Write about your family.**

1 What does your mother do in the morning? _____

2 What does your father do in the evening? _____

What **does** he/she **do**?	He/She **is** a nurse.
Where does he/she **work**?	He/She **works** at a hospital.
What do your sisters **do**?	They**'re** (They **are**) nurses.

1 Look. Circle and complete the dialogs.

Pete | Uncle – waiter | Dad – firefighter | Mom – cashier | Katrina | cousin – student | cousin – student

1 **Katrina:** What **do / does** your father do?

Pete: He's a _____.

Katrina: Where **do / does** he work?

Pete: He **work / works** at a fire station.

2 **Pete:** What **do / does** your cousins do?

Katrina: They are _____.

Pete: Where **do / does** they study?

Katrina: They **study / studies** at a college.

3 **Katrina:** _____

Pete: He's a waiter.

Katrina: _____

Pete: He _____ at a restaurant.

4 **Katrina:** _____

Pete: She's a cashier.

Katrina: _____

Pete: She works at a supermarket.

What **does** he/she **have to** do?	He/She **has to** feed the fish.
What **do** you/we/they **have to** do?	I/We/You/They **have to** feed the fish.

1 **Look. Complete the questions and answers.**

All tasks
May 14th
Matt to do: feed the cat twice today
Lucy and David to do: clean their rooms
Lucy and I to do: do the dishes
Lucy to do: practice the piano after school

1 **A:** What does Matt have to do?

B: He _____.

2 **A:** What do Lucy and David have to do?

B: They _____.

3 **A:** What _____ Lucy and I _____?

B: You _____.

4 **A:** What _____ Lucy _____?

B: She _____.

I/You/We/They	**always** **usually**	do the dishes.
He/She	**sometimes** **never**	takes out the trash.

2 **Look. Write never, usually, or always.**

Everyday Habits	Mon	Tues	Wed	Thurs	Fri
1 We _____ eat a good breakfast.	✓	✓	✓	✓	✓
2 She _____ plays tennis after school.					
3 I _____ wake up late.	✓	✓	✓	✓	

What **can** a penguin do?	It **can** swim. It **can't** fly.	subject + *can/can't* + verb
What **can** bears do?	They **can** climb. They **can't** fly.	
Can a penguin swim?	Yes, it **can**.	subject + *can/can't*
Can bears fly?	No, they **can't**.	

1 Write one animal name in each box in the chart.

> a bear   a camel   a snake   lizards   penguins   sea lions

What Can They Do?	Can	Can't
1 live in ice and snow		
2 do tricks		
3 live in deserts		

2 Look at 1. Complete the dialogs.

1 A: _____ a penguin _____ in ice and snow?

B: Yes, _____, but a camel _____.

3 A: What _____ a camel _____?

B: _____ live in deserts.

5 A: _____ a bear live in forests?

B: _____.

2 A: What can lizards do?

B: They _____ live in deserts.

4 A: Can a bear live in deserts?

B: No, it _____.

6 A: What _____ sea lions _____?

B: Sea lions _____ tricks, but they _____ talk.

| What **is** the weather like today? | It**'s** hot and sunny. |
| What **was** the weather **like** yesterday? | It **was** sunny. We **were** warm. |

1 Look. Complete the questions and answers.

Carla

Barcelona, Spain	
Yesterday	Today

32°C	32°C

Massi

Algiers, Algeria	
Yesterday	Today

23°C	20°C

Yoko

Sapporo, Japan	
Yesterday	Today
10°C	5°C

1 **Massi:** What _____ the weather like today in Barcelona?

Carla: It _____ hot and rainy.

2 **Yoko:** What _____ the weather like yesterday in Algiers?

Massi: It _____ warm and cloudy.

3 **Carla:** _____ today in Sapporo?

Yoko: _____

2 Look at **1**. Complete the dialogs.

1 **A:** _____

B: It was hot and sunny.

2 **A:** What is the weather like today in Algiers?

B: _____

3 **A:** What was the weather like in Sapporo yesterday?

B: _____

| How **does** the apple pie taste? | It **tastes** delicious. |
| How **do** your new shoes **feel**? | They **feel** good. |

1 **Look. Match the words and write the sentences.**

1  **2**  **3**  **4**

1 The flowers   looks   awful. _____

2 The cheese   smell   tight. _____

3 The shoes   look   nice. _____

4 The shirt   smells   comfortable. _____

2 **Write the questions.**

1 **A:** _____

B: The music sounds nice.

2 **A:** _____

B: The cookies taste delicious.

3 **A:** _____

B: The scarf feels soft.

4 **A:** _____

B: The perfume smells nice.

Is there **any** pizza?	Yes, there is **some** pizza.	Are there **any** onions?	Yes, there are **some** onions.
Is there **any** fish?	No, there isn't **any** fish.	Are there **any** eggs?	No, there aren't **any** eggs.

1 **Look and write.**

Special Today!

bread
cucumber
lettuce
mustard

2 **Look at 1. Write some or any.**

1 There is _____ lettuce.

2 There isn't _____ tomato sauce.

3 There aren't _____ tomatoes.

4 There are _____ cucumbers.

3 **Write questions and answers. Then draw the sandwich.**

1 Are there _____ bananas?

Yes, there are _____ bananas.

2 _____ onions?

No, there aren't _____ onions.

3 _____ yogurt?

_____ yogurt.

4 _____ chips?

_____ chips.

Silly Sandwich

Did you/he/she/they get enough sleep yesterday?	Yes, I/he/she/they did.	No, I/he/she/they didn't

1 **Read and match.**

1 Did you have   **a** to the zoo?

2 Did they eat   **b** Sue ride their bikes?

3 Did she go   **c** you see any rocks?

4 Did he   **d** a healthy lunch?

5 Did   **e** visit a museum?

6 Did Al and   **f** fun?

2 **Look. Write questions and answers.**

1 **A:** Did Matt eat any breakfast?

   B: No, _____.

2 **A:** _____ enough sleep?

   B: No, _____.

3 **A:** Did Sue have a big breakfast?

   B: Yes, _____.

4 **A:** _____ some exercise?

   B: Yes, _____.

Where **did** you/he/she/they **go**?	I/He/She/They **went** to the Science Museum.	
What **did** you/he/she/they **see**?	I/He/She/They **saw** an interesting movie about dinosaurs.	
Did you/he/she/they **like** it?	Yes, I/he/she/they **liked** it.	No, I /he/she/they **didn't like** it.

1 **Find and circle the past form of the verbs. Then match.**

l	g	r	d	r	a	n	k	z		**1**	eat
a	t	e	m	z	m	l	k	o		**2**	do
p	o	n	h	a	d	x	u	i		**3**	drink
i	n	e	h	r	g	d	i	d		**4**	get
a	f	g	c	g	o	t	s	w		**5**	have
z	x	c	v	b	r	o	d	e		**6**	ride

2 **Look and circle. Then answer.**

Jeff and Jack

Tim

1 Where did Jeff and Jack **go** / **went** yesterday? _____

2 What did they **see** / **saw**? _____

3 Where **does** / **did** Tim go last weekend? _____

4 **Does** / **Did** Tim like it? _____

Young Learners English Practice Movers: Listening A

– 5 questions –

 192

Listen and draw lines. There is one example.

Mary   John   Vicky   Fred

Jack   Sally

Young Learners English Practice Movers: Listening B

– 5 questions –

 Listen and check (✔) the box. There is one example.

What is his job?

A ☐

B ✔

C ☐

1 What is her job?

A ☐

B ☐

C ☐

2 What time does she usually stop working?

A ☐

B ☐

C ☐

Young Learners English Practice Movers: Listening B

3 What does she have to do every day?

 **A** ☐

 **B** ☐

 **C** ☐

4 What does she like about her job?

 **A** ☐

 **B** ☐

 **C** ☐

5 What job would she like to have in the future?

 **A** ☐

 **B** ☐

 **C** ☐

– 5 questions –

Listen and write. There is one example.

Susie's School Trip

What Susie did today: _____ *went on a school trip* _____

1 Where she went: _____

2 What she did in the morning: _____

3 What she had for lunch: _____

4 What she did in the afternoon: _____

5 What she learned: _____

Young Learners English Practice Movers: Reading & Writing A

Read the text. Choose the correct words and write them on the lines.

Example Bears live in many different kinds of places around the _____world_____. Some bears live in forests and mountains. Grizzly bears, for example, live in the Rocky Mountains, in the United States. They explore when

1 the _____ is warm and they sleep during the long winter. They

2 _____ climb trees and catch fish.

Polar bears live in the Arctic, where

3 it's _____ and cold all year

4 round. They have thick _____ to protect them from the cold and they

5 hunt for fish under the _____. Like all other bears, they fit right into their environment.

Example ocean desert world

1 weather water world

2 can should will

3 snowy hot rainy

4 feathers beaks fur

5 rock ice wood

Young Learners English Practice Movers: Reading & Writing B

– 6 questions –

Read the story. Choose a word from the box. Write the correct word next to numbers 1–6. There is one example.

Today starts off like any other day for Paul. He _____ wakes up _____ and gets out of bed. Then he goes into the bathroom and ¹_____. After that, he ²_____ and takes the bus to school. But something is different today. At lunch, he doesn't have to wait in line. The other kids let him go to the front. After school, Paul comes home. He usually has to ³_____ and take him for a walk, but today his sister does it for him. In the evening, Paul's mom cooks his favorite dinner. He always has to ⁴_____ after dinner, but today he gets a break. Instead of doing chores, he gets to ⁵_____ with his brother and sister. What's different about today? It's Paul's birthday. He almost always ⁶_____ at 8 o'clock, but today his parents let him stay up late and eat ice cream. "I wish every day was like today," says Paul.

Example

wakes up	eats breakfast	play soccer
do the dishes	does homework	goes to bed
washes his face	feed the dog	play games

(7) Now choose the best name for the story.

Check (✔) one box.

My Everyday Life ☐

A Very Special Day ☐

Time for a Break ☐

Young Learners English Practice Movers: Reading & Writing C

Look and read. Write *yes* or *no*.

Examples

It's cold and windy today. _____ *no*

People are watching a play. _____ *yes*

Questions

1 A woman is jogging.   _____

2 A family is having a picnic.   _____

3 There are some sandwiches on a plate. _____

4 A girl is walking her dog.   _____

5 People are watching a movie.   _____

6 There is some lemonade for sale.   _____

Young Learners English Practice Movers: Speaking B

Wordlist

Unit 1	Page
do my homework	4
eat breakfast	4
get dressed	4
go home	4
go to school	4
go to the park	4
home	4
play soccer	4
play video games	4
wake up	4
watch TV	4
seven thirty	5
time	5
brush your teeth	6
face	6
morning	6
like	7
put on his shoes	7
afternoon	8
evening	8
game	8
seven fifty	8
bike	9
ride	9
bacteria	10
cough	10
decay	10
germ	10
healthy	10
sick	10
sneeze	10
take a shower	10
wash your hands	10
time zone	14
subject	16
verb	16
bone	17
cake	17
note	17
shape	17

Unit 2	Page
cashier	20
farmer	20

firefighter	20
nurse	20
police officer	20
scientist	20
student	20
waiter	20
college	21
farm	21
fire station	21
hospital	21
laboratory	21
police station	21
store	21
school	24
fashion designer	26
gallery	26
landscape	26
photographer	26
sketch	26
donate	30
proud	30
Spain	31
skates	33
ski	33
skin	33
smart	33
smile	33
smoke	33
space	33
spoon	33
star	33
stop	33
storm	33

Unit 3	Page
chores	36
clean my room	36
do the dishes	36
feed the fish	36
make my bed	36
practice the piano	36
study for a test	36
take out the trash	36
walk the dog	36
always	37

day	37
twins	37
sometimes	37
say	38
alarm clock	39
never	39
usually	41
amount	42
cents	42
earn	42
euro	42
pocket money	42
subtotal	42
times	42
total	42
goat	47
noodles	47
capital letters	48
title	48
boy	49
joy	49
May	49
pay	49
ray	49
soy	49
toy	49

Unit 4	Page
animal	58
bear	58
camel	58
deer	58
lizard	58
owl	58
penguin	58
sea lion	58
shark	58
toucan	58
ice and snow	59
lake	59
rain forest	59
trick	60
well	60
bottom of the ocean	64

camouflage	64
chameleon	64
eat	64
polar bear	64
rock	64
stone	64
stonefish	64
tree bark	64
tree frog	64
canary	68
goldfish	68
hamster	68
million	68
parakeet	68
topic sentence	70
bean	71
boil	71
coin	71
foe	71
meat	71
oil	71
peach	71
tea	71
toe	71

Unit 5	Page
cloudy	74
cold	74
cool	74
hot	74
rainy	74
snowy	74
sunny	74
today	74
warm	74
windy	74
coat	75
raincoat	75
sandals	75
scarf	75
shorts	75
sunglasses	75
sweater	75
hike	76
snack	76

yesterday	76	block	103	dream	125	zoo	144
average	80	blow	103	drive	125	had	145
climate	80	flag	103	frog	125	interesting	145
extreme	80	flip-flops	103	grass	125	saw	145
opposite	80	fly	103	prince	125	went	145
temperature	80	glad	103	prize	125	learned	146
tourist	80	glass	103	troll	125	liked	146
sleep	81	glow	103			old	146
cricket	84	plant	103	**Unit 8**	**Page**	got	147
sled	84	play	103	healthy	128	walked	147
detail sentences	86	plum	103	any	129	ate	149
swim	86			enough	129	beautiful	150
scar	87	**Unit 7**	**Page**	unhealthy	130	boring	150
scout	87	bread	112	bad	131	colorful	150
slim	87	cucumbers	112	active	134	French	150
slow	87	from	112	activities	134	funny	150
snail	87	green	112	body	134	hand	150
swan	87	lettuce	112	calorie	134	scary	150
		mushrooms	112	measure	134	strange	150
Unit 6	**Page**	olives	112	put on weight	134	Flamenco	154
awful	90	onions	112	ball	138	Vietnam	155
delicious	90	peppers	112	call	138	object	156
feel	90	tomato sauce	112	footvolley	138	ant	157
flowers	90	turkey	112	hockey	138	band	157
horrible	90	fridge	114	net	138	chest	157
look	90	surprise	115	octopush	138	child	157
nice	90	blood	118	pumpkin	138	cold	157
pie	90	bone	118	race	138	fast	157
smell	90	brain	118	throw	138	nest	157
soft	90	energy	118	claw	141	plant	157
sound	90	muscles	118	draw	141	sand	157
soup	90	skin	118	haul	141	tent	157
sweet	90	vitamin	118	tall	141		
taste	90	Australia	122	wall	141		
terrible	90	donut	122	yawn	141		
tight	90	fried eggs	122				
cold	93	Japan	122	**Unit 9**	**Page**		
danger	93	Mexico	122	aquarium	144		
avoid	96	Spain	122	art gallery	144		
brain	96	butter	124	concert hall	144		
echo	96	maple syrup	124	dairy farm	144		
information	96	pancake	124	museum	144		
tongue	96	brick	125	national park	144		
final sentence	102	cream	125	school trip	144		
black	103	cry	125	theater	144		

ask a question with:

What time...

ask a question with:

When...

ask a question with:

in the morning / afternoon / evening

ask a question with:

at ____:____ (time)

ask a question with:

before work

ask a question with:

after work

answer with:

I...

answer with:

I always...

answer with:

I usually...

answer with:

I sometimes...

answer with:

I never...

answer with:

I have to...

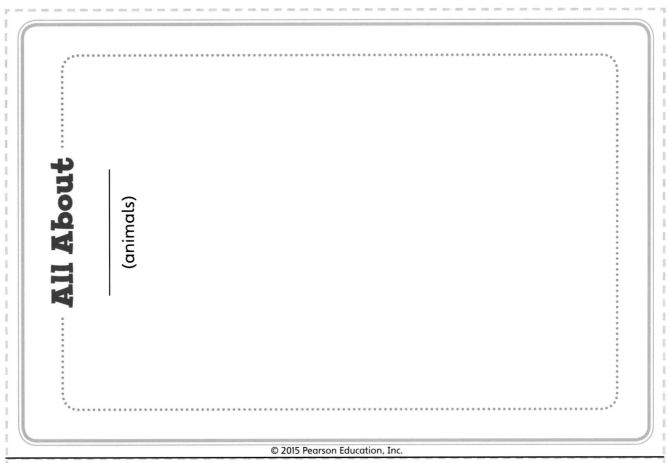

All About

_____
(animals)

© 2015 Pearson Education, Inc.

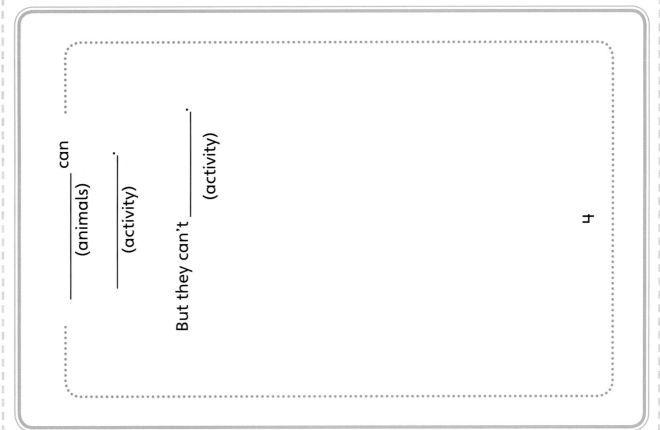

_____ can
(animals)

_____ .
(activity)

But they can't _____ .
(activity)

4

2

_____ live in

(animals)

_____ .

(habitat)

It's _____ there.

(weather word)

3

_____ eat

(animals)

_____ .

(food)

Dialog 2

A: Did you eat breakfast this morning?

B: Yes, it was awesome. Sharks are cool!

A: Did you like it?

B: I ate turkey and lettuce.

A: What did you do there?

B: Yes, I had eggs on toast. I'm ready for the baseball game!

A: What did you eat for dinner?

B: We went to the aquarium.

A: Where did you go yesterday?

B: We saw a movie about sharks.

3

My BIG ENGLISH World

My name: _____

My age: _____

My address: _____

My family: _____

ME

FOLD

©2015 Pearson Education, Ltd.

ENGLISH
AROUND ME

Look around you. Paste or draw things with English words. Write everyday words.

Everyday Words

_____

_____

_____

_____

MOVIE TICKET

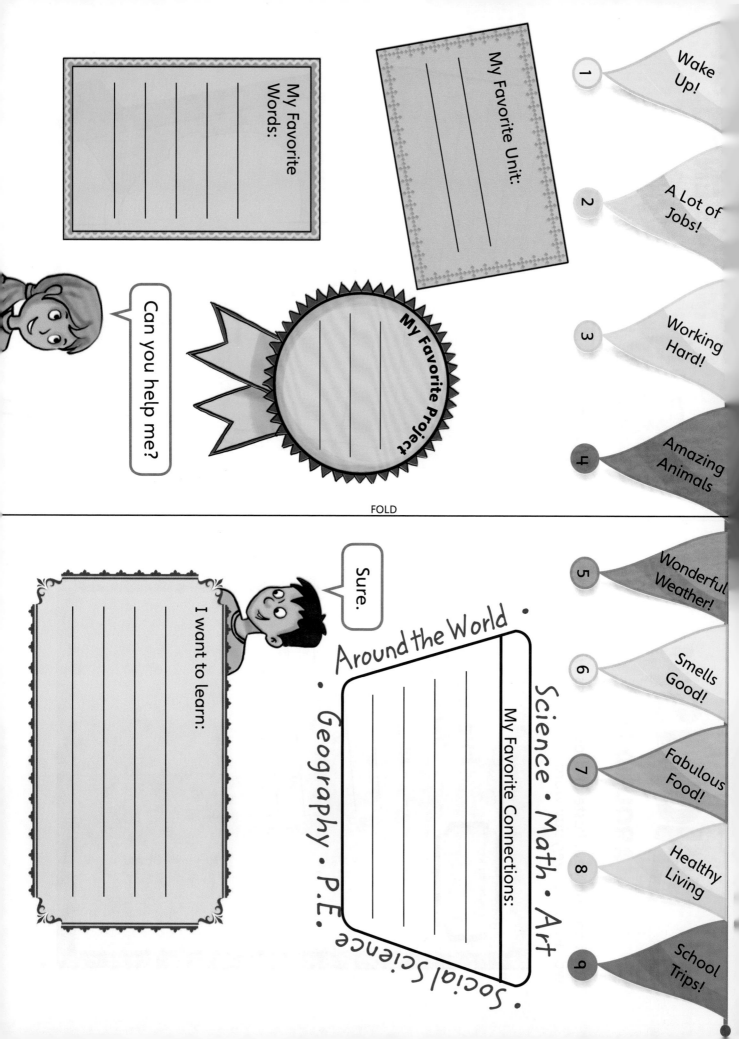

Unit 1, page 5

Unit 2, page 19

Unit 3, page 33

Unit 4, page 49